Paola Fraschini

Like the Lion and the Butterfly

Set Free the Energy and Talent Inside of You

D0896740

"It's more difficult to live than to die," my grandfather always told me.

From him I've learnt that defeat doesn't exist.
Losers are the ones that don't even reach failure, the ones that never fight, the ones that never risk anything.

My grandpa would have loved to write a book and visit Canada. Now that I'm in America I can do nothing but write it myself. For him, but most of all for you, because what I have learnt in these years could be an inspiration to help you reach your goals.

Paola Fraschini, *Like the Lion and the Butterfly.*
Set Free the Energy and Talent Inside of You

Editing and editorial project by Barbara Zippo
www.barbarazippo.net

On the front page: Paola Fraschini
Photo credit: Thomas Hubener
Clothes: Design Kontrol
Roller skates: Risport Skates and Roll Line

ISBN 9791220045896
ISBN 9791220045902

First Italian edition *"Come il leone e la farfalla"*, October
2018
English translation: Federica Bellante Elman
Editor: Barbara Zippo
Assistant editor: Kerry Vera Lea

Don't forget to write your review on the Amazon sales
page of the book *"Like The Lion and the Butterfly"*
and if you want to keep in touch with me, visit:
Website - sign up for the blog - newsletter: http://www.paolafraschini.com/
Instagram: https://www.instagram.com/paola_fraschini/
Facebook: https://www.facebook.com/paola.fraschini/

Index

Preface

By Max Gentile

From the first time I met Paola, I understood that I had in front of me a determined and humble girl who was eager to grow up. She joined me as a guest speaker during one of my courses. In the years to follow, our contact became more frequent, almost as if there was a connection between us that little by little became like a thick and resistant rope made of trust, affection and mutual honesty.

I've noticed that what for others are external walls, for Paola represented inner obstacles that step by step she has transformed into victories with her sweet stubbornness.

I guessed that her biggest difficulty would come once her skating career ended so I was more focused on Paola "the person" rather than Paola "the skater."

She had won so many World Championships, that to make everything smoother when the time came, I started to open up a few doors on our path together.

Athletes that don't reason preventatively, can suffer from mental traumas periodically.

I remember when after a timeline (an exercise of visual representations of events in chronological order) she kept telling me: "I want a musical, I want to skate and act."

There was confusion, but little by little we worked together to get rid of the fog and see a future. She was constantly amazing, full of revelations that with attention were used to analyze, observe and consequently manage through her perspicacity. I felt we were close to success and, luckily, she believed in "signs" that life gave her like instruments to light up her journey.

This is not a book about skating.

By reading Paola's story, you will understand how to build up a winning mental mindset, in sports and in life. You will find facts and strategies to replicate in your everyday life even if you have never worn skates before.

You will discover that sacrifice is understood only as such when you are not in line with yourself and you haven't decided which direction to take.

Paola will explain how to overcome blocks with efficient motivational "pills" throughout her story.

We live in a society where, in the majority of cases, we are nearly forced to be somebody else. We fear abandonment, refusal and judgement.

Paola has decided to be who she really is, not the one that others want or expect her to be. She is the type of person that demonstrates with her teachings that we can either live a life full of excuses, content with ourselves, or thrive in the true essence that is who we are.

I always thought changing was inevitable because we are all in constant evolution. We only need to decide if we want to suffer from it or create it.

To evolve, it is necessary to start from loving yourself, not by external recognition. With this attitude, obstacles will stop being obstacles and will become opportunities.

Paola exemplifies this perfectly with her mind, but even more so, with her heart. She creates her life with patience, power and direct attention. She didn't make excuses to stop, but only good motivation to continue her mission.

She chose to be guided by her most intimate essence, the one that everyone has, she decided to listen to herself and let go of her fears.

She could have had a million reasons to give up her skating career: a small skating rink in bad condition, being far from a good skating center, the frequent trips, the injuries, the lack of finances and the abominable distance of affection, but she has never stopped.

By reading her inspiring words, I hope that you can apply what Paola has put into practice to reach your true potential.

Introduction

While browsing a magazine my eyes met this quote:

"The biggest thing lacking in your life is to not express your true identity. Say who you are."

I'm an anonymous artistic roller skating champion. I have practiced this sport since I was a child. I've been an athlete on the Italian national team since 1996. My natural shyness and the sport itself don't help popularity. I believe roller skating is a complete sport and incredibly spectacular, but it is silent, non-Olympic, nearly unknown because it's not on ice but on wheels and it is not recognized by the military forces, as is usually the case for other sports. Despite this, it boasts an Italian national team admired around the world, world champions throughout the years and athletes and coaches at the highest levels.

Having said this, to continue to cultivate my passion I always had to fund skating with other professional activities. In Genoa, skating rinks aren't the best. I've always asked myself: "Why do I do this? Personal satisfaction?" That's certainly not missing, but it's not enough!

Although roller skating is a sport known as "minor," that doesn't mean it's easier or less challenging than other sports. It's actually for this reason that the sacrifice behind it is higher. It's always in the most difficult situations that you must go deep and ask what the true meaning of everything really is.

The answer is: I skate simply because when I'm skating, I feel priceless emotions. I love to dance, to feel my body moving with the rhythm of the music, to express myself through this "channel" and let the "real me" out. It's amazing to feel my body harmoniously doing what I tell it to do and to be in a particular dimension that experts call "flow." It's like being in a soap bubble floating light on the skating rink. I skate for this reason, not for money, or simply because I like it, but for a deeper meaning that today I define as "holy."

Skating forced me to look deeply into myself and look in the eyes of my limitations, weaknesses and fears; I had to face up to every competition in a new way. I have learnt and studied techniques that have allowed me to evolve and discover many different sides of my personality. Along the way, I have met people that have taken my hands and guided me through and towards my personal realization.

Athletes are a bit like warriors: to face a competition is like going down onto the battlefield. Most of all, they have to overcome fears and resistance. Preparation is long, it's made of intense phases of training and others of rest, and in the middle of this your mood is not constantly stable. It's not always possible to separate your personal life from your sport. Everything is interconnected and can influence your performance. It's a very delicate balance and finding a winning formula is not easy. I've lived through and experienced all of this and I know full well what it means to face such a journey and what sacrifices it may involve.

Through my story you can make your preparation effective due to mental techniques that I used for myself to reach my targets and win competitions. You will learn to balance your energy and manage your time to be effective.

Some techniques in particular have literally changed my life allowing me to achieve incredible results. Remember that if you are only physically training, you should know that you are not using 100% of your potential.

Mind and body cannot be split, changing the codes of your mind mean changing your life.

There is, however, a rule: it is necessary to be ready to question yourself and work with a lot of patience. There are no shortcuts. You will understand by reading my story that it won't be easy, but it is certainly possible.

Imagine a walk in the mountains where you face ascents, descents, obstacles and precipices. You can stop, take the time you need, start again and see beautiful landscapes, but then you will have to face the difficult parts.

To get to the summit you have to take that first step, have the courage to get moving and strip yourself of everything that no longer belongs to you!

Remember that a sport is a game of attack; you enter into the field, put fear aside and go right to the target.

Playing small does not serve the world. You were born to shine, to manifest what is already within you.

I started out as a common skater and today I perform as one of the main characters in the show *Volta, by Cirque du Soleil*. I've learned a lot in these years and, as a World Champion, I don't want my titles to fall into oblivion in the future. I wish instead to share the experience and practical tools that I made mine.

References to my history will be functional to the presentation of useful techniques to guide you to your goals more quickly and effectively. Facing the challenges and knowing your potential will be easier because you will acquire an attitude that will allow you to see the world in a new light. With this book, I want to convey that once you have discovered what you are passionate about, you can live the extraordinary experience of becoming fully yourself. Whether it be sports, art, a combination, or any way of expressing yourself, self-expression is an incredibly healthy way to achieve a full state of self-awareness and realization.

Only you know what your dream is!
Believe in the possibility of making it happen and be willing
to take risks for it.

Chapter 1

My Skating Club, Initial Training and Adolescence

I love dancing. Since I was a child I used to lock myself in the bedroom, put the music on at full volume and dance. It was my own time when I was able to express my feelings. The music was in me and I was letting it out through a part of myself. I used to dance to every single cartoon soundtrack. My family was the audience. I didn't do this to be appreciated but simply because I wanted to be connected with the most authentic part of myself.

My mother is an artistic skating coach. On my crib, instead of a holy image as people normally do, she hung a little skate. Was I blessed by this? Was it given to me as a sign? Who knows? But skates always attracted me. At the age of two I was rolling around in my Fisher Price skates and I didn't want to take them off. My mom has never forced me. I wanted to skate, to dance, to jump, to wear a tutu and most of all, to compete.

It started as a game and little by little things became more serious, when the first competitions began. I still remember all the steps of my first routine with choreography to a Russian musical piece. I was wearing a white and red dress and I was feeling very happy.

I was a shy girl, I didn't talk that much. I liked to be with children the same age as me but I also liked to be on my own. I liked to play with Barbie dolls, invent stories and live in my own magical universe... but in the skating rink I used to transform myself! That still happens today.

Everyone used to say: "Paola you are a different person in the skating rink."

Was the one in the rink the "real" Paola? Today I can say it certainly was. Back then I didn't realize it and I didn't know what they meant when they asked if that was the "real me." For me, it was natural to interpret something like music and put a part of myself into it.

Despite the judges, the competitions have always been somewhere I could express myself freely and fully. I could be fun, sensual, ridiculous, serious or angry in a context that doesn't involve any embarrassment.

It's the time when I listen to myself and I let myself out. I want to be that Paola in real life and to be able to do that I need to unveil certain parts of me like thoughts, prejudices, judgments and fears.

Society nowadays is forcing us to interpret roles that are not true to ourselves and, growing up, we forget about our essence, our talent and our life's mission. Uncountable influences from our family, friends, relatives, teachers and religions take us away from our true nature. We don't recognize ourselves and, along the way, we lose our purpose.

Skating has always been here to remind me of who I am and who I can be. It gave me the opportunity to be in contact with my soul, with the best part of myself. It gave me the opportunity to dive deeper into my feelings to show me my limits and my fears but also my authenticity. Skating has always been more than a sport: it's the teacher that guided my life.

The deepest fear is to be powerful through overcoming every limit. It's your light that makes you more fearful, not your shadow.

Sturla Pattinaggio Genova

When I was five years old, my mom opened the skating club *Sturla Pattinaggio Genova* of which my grandpa was the president. Only a few skaters were a part of it and, with my mother's professionalism and consistency, the club grew. Today it has about 150 skaters despite the difficulties that go with the territory. It's incredibly difficult to find a good place to skate in Genoa! From ages seven to twelve, I used to skate in Piazzale Kennedy, near the sea. It was an outdoor space of 8,611 square feet. The changing room was an empty shipping container and we were in the middle of a circus camp with animals and gypsies all over the place.

After every training session I used to have black hands from the dirt and dust. I used to clean myself with wipes as we didn't even have a bathroom. Sometimes we used to train in *Piscine di Albaro*, in the parking space at the entrance of the center. Falling on the concrete wasn't a nice experience!

Later on, they let us train in *Pista del Baretto* for few hours a week. Compared to the others it was better and it's where the team still trains today.

Pista del Baretto is an outdoor space, small and very different from the competition rinks. To avoid the rain, we used to move to *Carlini*, a sort of garage with columns in the middle where after an hour of training, my eyes used to be very swollen because of the dust.

I grew up like this, fighting for what I loved. I was the Cinderella that used to put a nice dress on for the competitions but used to skate only when it was possible and in extreme situations. But everyone in my club was committed to it, to bringing the passion to it. After all, the competitions were not going bad at all.

At that time, I used to skate individually and also in pairs with Marco Noli, with whom I won my first national competitions. In 1996 we entered the National Team and won our first European competition in Freiburg. Those first results made us forget all the sacrifices of that whole year.

Sports and Adolescence

Everything was going really well and skating for me wasn't so intense until, around the age of fourteen, something changed.

I used to finish school around 1 o'clock, do my homework on the way home, eat lunch, then homework again and by 2:30 I was already skating. I used to study in between training sessions. It wasn't a heavy schedule for me, it was like a routine. The life of an athlete is easy until adolescence, then there comes the time when you see your friends going out on the weekends while you are at training.

You suddenly open your eyes and you feel different. You would like to be free and like everyone else. You wish to compare yourself to your peers... it's an incredibly challenging and confusing time for an athlete.

It happened to me and right at that time my skating career had a drop. I always say that whoever continues over seventeen years of age will surely reach the end. For the clubs, every year is the same: many teenagers will leave. They have school commitments and first loves, or they wish to meet friends more often and so they abandon the sport.

We tend to repress what belongs to childhood and experiment with new things. Is it worth it?

To abandon the sport you practice the most, means you miss the train... probably forever! To skip one or two years of a competitive sport means not being able to go back to the same level as before and it's a shame. At twenty-five years old you wish you could go back but it's too late. I'm not saying you shouldn't enjoy the events that that age has to offer you, but it's good to have balance in every aspect of your life.

Before quitting something you are passionate about that has been part of your life since childhood, you need to think about it carefully because when you decide to quit a sport, what you have developed is unfortunately lost forever.

Regarding my experience, around the age of sixteen I decided to quit individual figure skating to dedicate myself to dance couple. Our target was to qualify for the Junior World Championships and we did. The 2001 competition was being held in Florence. There was a big buzz around about it and even my school friends decided to come and see me while they were on a school trip.

When you compete in pairs you have to establish a deep understanding, become "one" and support each other completely. I have known Marco Noli since I was born and to compete with him has always been easy for me. He was rational and calm and I was emotional and passionate. We used to compensate for one and other and we were close like brother and sister.

During the World Championships, I was so nervous and didn't know any relaxation techniques. At first, we were overcome with anxiety and weren't expressing ourselves fully but once we got more into it, we had a great competition. We had a good original dance and a great free dance but it wasn't enough. We came in first in total score and second in placement (in that case placement was more important).

I was destroyed. We missed the gold medal by a whisker. I went up to the second placement podium in tears during the medal ceremony. I saw the situation as full of injustice and bad luck. At the end of the competition my mother came up to me and told me: "Paola, your journey is still long, this is just the beginning, you will win the World Championship one day, I promise!"

I have always believed in her words. For me she is a guide, a mentor and an example. She knows how to approach me, she recognizes my every emotion, she can read through me even if I'm not talking and those words, that day, touched me deeply. I didn't know how to reach the target but I knew that one day I would reach it. "Everything has a time, don't hurry jumping the stages," she always told me, and there is nothing truer than this.

Everything in life comes when you are ready to receive it. Perhaps if I had won that competition, my mom's words wouldn't have influenced me like that. In the following years, I always fought and believed in what my mother had envisioned for me. So many times, even today, when I wish to receive something but I'm not ready for it, I realize that I still need to take another step, that there's still one more journey to prepare myself for the right moment.

It's like the universe knows the route, sometimes we need to trust someone wiser than us.

That World Championship left me with a good energy. When I came back home, friends and relatives were there waiting for me to celebrate. After such a remarkable experience even oral exams at school became easy, my grades at school were better and I had the impression that I was more mature not only in skating but also in my personal life.

When high school was over, I was dreaming of becoming an actress but I didn't know how to pursue this career. When I was nineteen, the internet was not widespread like it is today and I believed that to become an actress I had to move to America, ignoring that I had one of the best drama schools in Italy on my doorstep. My parents were always questioning if that was the right decision, especially if I wanted to have a family in the future. I was confused and demoralized and I didn't know what to do.

DAMS- a university course in music, art and drama- was the only one close to what I was interested in and the best course was in Bologna. There was a question haunting me: "What will I be able to achieve after I graduate?"

At that time in Italy there was the conception that you needed to have a permanent job. "You are a woman, family is important, to be a teacher is the best career because you are busy during the morning and you can stay at home with your children in the afternoon. If you are lucky enough to have a permanent position you are guaranteed a good salary, maternity leave, holidays and sick pay."

I knew my family was saying this because they wanted to reassure me and wanted the best for me, but all of these opinions influenced my ideas so much that becoming an actress or going to *DAMS* seemed crazy. I convinced myself that if I pursued that dream, I would be condemned to a life of hardships, always looking for a temporary job. And of course, family: how would I cope with children?

In this state of total confusion, I used to spend my days reading the university's leaflets, I knew them inside and out, as well as the content of every single exam.

I could be a good doctor, but that needs to be in your nature! Maybe I can become a psychologist... for sure I don't want to do law or engineering.

I think economics is quite boring but they say it's easy to find a job once you graduate. Maybe I could try...? My head was full of questions and I had to evaluate every pro and con.

One day I decided to attend a class at the University of Economics. I ran away after half an hour. I have a great sense of duty, even if I don't like something, and I know I have to do it, I carry it on until the end. If I had decided to do economics I probably would have ended up with good grades, even if I wasn't interested in it at all!

We fear the future and planning makes us feel safe. To have direction is certainly important, but isn't the beauty in life the constant change and a bit of unpredictability? At that time, I didn't know and I thought the security of a permanent job like all my friends had would let me lead a peaceful life. Inside, I was wondering why I wasn't born with clear ideas. My friends knew they wanted to become dentists, doctors or architects... Why wasn't I like them?

The idea of becoming an actress or working in show business wasn't considered *normal*. No university had these kind of studies in Genoa and as everyone was asking, "What kind of life would you lead?"

I then decided to apply for other universities. I applied for medical studies, psychology and sports studies.

But, in September, I missed all the admission tests because I had the European Championships in dance couple, the last with my partner Marco Noli, with whom I had now skated with for twelve years. So I decided to apply for Biology because it didn't have any admission tests. I liked all the subjects, I passed all the exams with good grades but I felt that the life of a biologist wasn't for me.

Why not try something else? This idea of "What to do when you grow up?" used to be stuck in my mind.

I spent a whole year trying to understand what my journey could have been.

I abandoned the idea of show business as I thought there wasn't an opportunity for me, but there was nothing else I really liked.

One day at the university, a friend told me she was going to try the admission test for Physical Therapy: a three-year course, many exams from Biology were recognized and there were plenty of job opportunities.

I couldn't believe it! It was the solution that I was waiting for! I could work with athletes, and maybe find a part time job and help my mother with the skating club. It seemed that everything would suddenly work.

It was exactly what others envisioned for me. Finally, like all my friends, I had a purpose in life!

Study, graduate and have a family. I had a boyfriend for two years and things were going well. A serious guy, an engineer, he could have been "the one."

I had lost a bit of interest in skating as Marco had decided to end his skating career and I was now alone. So I started to dedicate my time to *Solo Dance*, a new type of speciality that was becoming popular among many skaters. I competed and came in third place at the National Championships and qualified for the European Cup at the end of the summer.

But, I had a sense of sadness having to compete alone;

I felt lonely in the middle of the skating rink as I was used to skating with someone else.

When the National Competition was over I had a little meltdown as I wasn't sure I was able to go through with the other competitions. My mom reassured me saying that time would help me to overcome that change.

During the summer of 2004 I started to intensely study for the physical therapy admission test. I knew it was going to be difficult to pass as only twenty-five students would be admitted to the course. I was determined in my choice: it truly looked like the right career for me.

In September I took the test and, while I was competing for the European Cup in Sardinia, the results came in. I received a call from a friend who told me that I was one-hundred-and-thirtieth in the list and I wasn't admitted to the course. All my university friends from Biology were admitted except for me. I was shocked, I was demoralized, I couldn't understand it and I was 100% sure I had done the test well.

When I came back from the competition I went to the university to ask for an explanation and see the test, but nobody really helped me. I was panicked, so I asked my dad for help and he called a lawyer. I wanted to understand what my mistakes were.

As soon as the university received the letter from the lawyer they called me back. They told me they had taken away ten points from my test by mistake. I qualified among the first twenty students in the whole region of Liguria! So, I was right, the test went well! I was very happy and I was convinced I had found my route.

After a couple of months of lessons and an internship, I immediately understood that my ideas about being a physical therapist were very different from the realities of

it. I believed I would be dealing with massages and rehabilitation for young athletes, but I was instead working in
a neurological clinic helping people with serious illnesses
to walk again.

When I came home from work I would often cry and,
as a result of a psychosomatic reaction, I had developed a
tremendous case of colitis.

Clearly it wasn't for me, but because I'm stubborn I
decided to finish at the university committing myself to
the maximum time and, in November 2007, I graduated
with honors.

Chapter 2
2008 The Crisis

I was a physical therapist, my boyfriend was an engineer and I was content to skate and reach a good place in the national competitions. I saw skating as a hobby, like going to the gym was for my friends. I wanted to deal with sports rehabilitation, the only aspect of physical therapy that interested me. I wasn't yet aware that my desire came from my need to be an integral part of the skating world and to become one of the best.

I started with an unpaid internship with a few sports physical therapists and in the morning I would work in a private clinic to earn some money. I'd train when I had time and I was helping my mom with the skating club. I also went to a jazz dance class that allowed me to explore new movements and expressions.

My days were full and I did everything I could to be efficient and find a route to the success I craved. I was looking for stability by imitating other people's lives and silencing my most real inner needs.

When you don't have the courage to listen to yourself, to your own desires and to your own weaknesses, sooner or later something will force you to step back and solve what is unsolvable.

There are moments of total confusion when you don't even know who you are and you can't see the light at the end of the tunnel. You wish to come out from it but you don't know how, and so in those moments, you find the courage to ask yourself questions you have ignored for so long.

Following the route of this inner journey, you are guided through the light, and once out, you look back and you understand that it was really necessary to go through that dark internal road.

You realize, at a certain point, that things will come only when you are ready to welcome them. You look back and you understand that every step, every choice, every single experience of your whole life makes sense depending on the present because you couldn't understand, you couldn't see, you couldn't catch the opportunity, you wouldn't be what you became without that journey. The mosaic is completed with the last piece and the design becomes clear.

Federica Loredan

This was what happened in 2008. The information on my identity card did not correspond to me at all.

For a long time, I believed I was someone I wasn't and at a certain point life gave me the bill and opened my eyes.

In July of that year, the Italian Championships were held in Trieste.

I wanted, at the least, to qualify for the European Cup, so I needed to finish in the top five. It was the last year males and females were competing together. I knew the podium would be composed wholly of males with only two available places for European Cup qualification remaining. After the compulsory dances, I was in seventh place, so I knew I was totally out of the game.

I did the free dance to the best of my abilities, I knew I had nothing to lose. I gained a position but it wasn't enough to qualify for the European Cup. I was sixth, the fifth was from Trieste. I was infuriated with myself and the entire situation. It was the only time I didn't show up to the medal ceremony. It was too much; I went away screaming. The anger I had inside had exploded, it wasn't fair, I deserved more.

I wanted to stop skating, I had enough. I was ending up in tears at the end of every competition. It wasn't a life. I was coming into the rink with the desire to do my best but it wasn't enough and once they were announcing scores and ranking I was always cut to the heart.

I came back home in the grip of anger and rancor. Something in my life had to change, I was at the end of myself, I couldn't handle it anymore. To increase the torment, unexpected news arrived.

The day after the competition my parents called me and my brother into the kitchen and they announced that they were separating. I went out the house banging the door. I hadn't yet gotten over the emotions of the night before, I was overwhelmed by a hurricane.

I wanted to escape, to throw everything in the air and scream. I grew up with family values and in one moment everything was falling apart in front of my eyes, and it was just the beginning of the wave of changes in my life.

I wanted to support my parents and be a support for my younger brother, but I had a wall in front of me every time I tried to go somewhere. I couldn't give sense to what I was doing, it was like swimming madly trying not to drown in sadness. A lot of questions were invading my mind. I wanted to put everything back in place but I couldn't.

I could do anything but stay close to my parents and try to comprehend my worries and fears.

We always think our parents are superheroes, perfect and invincible individuals. In these situations, we realize that they are human beings, with merits and defects and that they too can go through crisis, dark times and difficulties.

In the face of such situations it is necessary to come out of your shell and take the reins of your life.

My parents' separation inevitably opened my eyes regarding my own love story. In August we went on a vacation and I realized I was no longer happy with him: my energy was blocked. I needed to be free to start again with myself, despite his great goodness, he was no longer connected to who I wanted to become. To let go of a person I shared a lot with for five years generated a deep sense of emptiness.

My boyfriend was just a friend, a confidant, a lover and a pillar of certainty but I had decided that my points of reference had to change.

I wanted to create a state of mind to let go of the past and start back over again.

I broke up with him although it was clear that I would have to suffer a lot.

To evolve in life, it's usually necessary to let go of something or someone that doesn't belong to you anymore.
And it hurts.

At the end of October, I went to the Hettange Open International, a competition held in France for the sixth, seventh and eighth qualifiers at the Italian Championships. I've been part of that competition for years and it never excited me that much, but I had been summoned and I wanted to finish the year properly. It was the worst competition of my life. I was in bits. My body was trying so hard but my mind was elsewhere. I ranked fourth. I wanted to stop skating as I felt I couldn't express myself anymore. I had lost the freedom I'd always felt in my skates. I couldn't handle my tears at the end of every competition and I felt a huge disappointment.

I went back home without strength, convinced that I was going to quit skating once and for all.

But it wasn't over.

After two weeks, I received the bad news that my grandmother was dying. For me she was like a second mom. I grew up with her, I remember afternoons at my grandparents' house, vacations by the mountains and the competitions with her there. I adored her. Both of my grandparents were pure love for me and her in particular.

She always had a smile on her face and open arms to console me. By the time I went to the hospital it was too late, that smile was gone; I had lost her too.

My parents separated, my mom moved out of the house, I broke up with my boyfriend, and my beloved grandmother had gone. Within five months, each of my most important bonds were shattered. I felt a sense of emptiness and loneliness. I was literally broken into a thousand pieces.

Despite the fact that I wanted to quit skating after the competition in Hettange, I could not stop it, a call stronger than me dragged me back. It was the only thing that made me feel good. I used to train with the music *Lord of the Dance* by the Irish composer Roman Hardiman. I danced, tried and created. The notes entered into me and I let go of the emotions that I had been repressing for a long time. The skating rink was my secure place, I was alive while dancing.

It was a very intense period when, for the first time, I asked myself existential questions: What am I doing here? What is my purpose? What am I living for? What do I want to give to the world? What are my talents?

I used to read a lot. I was thirsty for answers and some certainty to lean on to give me a sense of what was happening to me.

I did research on religions and found out that the common idea behind all of them is that God is Love. I was impressed by it. Therefore, if God is Love, it means that to be in contact with Him I need to Love. Ok then, who and how?

Reading an article on the internet I found another quote. "If you try to invert the order of: "Love your neighbor as you love yourself" into "Love yourself as you love your neighbor," it would probably be more clear that if you don't love yourself you can't love others too. Learn to love yourself and then open up to the world."

This was the answer to so many of my tormenting doubts. I had to learn to love myself. That was the first step. In that moment I didn't love myself at all. I had let myself go, I became fat, I had acne, I didn't go out, I just wanted to relax and stay at home. My job didn't satisfy me, I was losing time and I couldn't give any sense to what I was doing.

I used to wake up without the desire to face the day, nothing gave me enough motivation to get up again from that feeling.

But one day while I was in the bathroom, I looked at myself in the mirror and something was different.

Where had my smile gone? My vitality? My energy?

Who had I become? I was ugly, I couldn't recognize myself anymore. For the first time after so many months, I didn't stop by just looking at my appearance. I went deep down and I told myself: "Paola, what do you want to do about your life?"

The first tears came down. Then I let out an irrepressible cry. I was freeing myself from the chains that had imprisoned my soul for too long. I probably cried for an hour and I was so exhausted that in the end I said with a weak but safe voice: "It's enough now, I deserve to be happy."

From that moment something had changed. I'm convinced that that decision was enough to make the ball spin in my direction:

Change the way you look at things and the things you look at change.

Wayne Dyer

People and situations that I met from that moment on seemed to adjust to the decision I took: I wanted to be happy. It was like the universe was waiting for me to express my decision, strong and clear to start working in my favor. I felt I needed a guide, a person that could help me to get out from that situation. So I picked up the phone and I called Doctor Anna Petritoli for a consultation.

Chapter 3
2009 The Rebirth

On a cold Wednesday in February of 2009, I went to my doctor, a specialist in gynecology among many other skills. I knew she would help me. While I was in the waiting room, looking at the view from the window, I thought that day was exactly like me in that moment of life: meaningless. The warm voice of the doctor broke off the contemplative silence.

"Good morning Paola! Nice to see you again! Come along please!"

"Good morning doctor, how are you? You look well."

"I'm good, thank you. Take a seat please. So what's up?" She asked me while looking at my face. "What is going on? Isn't your face swollen?"

"I think so doctor, I let myself go lately. It hasn't been a great period!" I answered with eyes full of tears... Her face changed expression.

"What is going on? Tell me. I don't know anything."

I mustered up the courage to tell her everything I had been holding onto for a while. "The last months haven't been easy; I went through some changes in my life... mostly regarding my relationships!" My throat was knotted, I couldn't continue, but the doctor encouraged me.

"Tell me, I'm here to help you!"

I took a breath and I continued. "My parents separated last summer."

"What?!" She interrupted me. "I'm really sorry, how come?"

"It happened very suddenly, I guess I didn't expect it. Initially I reacted well, I think I've done all I could to be close to everyone... Maybe now I'm paying for it. My parents' separation was only the beginning of a series of changes!" I answered with a broken voice.

"What do you mean?" The doctor asked me.

"Do you remember the guy I was with for five years? I broke up with him. I did it because my parents' separation opened my eyes. I understood that maybe I wasn't in love with him anymore."

"Well, it's good that you understood that... There are many love stories that continue even when everything has finished and then they fall apart when it's too late!"

"Yes, you are right doctor, I'm aware of it, but getting away from a person who has been a point of reference for five years it wasn't easy, especially considering what has happened to my parents!"

"I'm sure of this, dear Paola."

"On top of this I had a crush on someone recently... but because of me the whole thing was nipped in the bud!"

The doctor thought about this and paced the room.

"What do you mean, "because of me"?"

"I was insecure, I don't know, I liked him but I didn't have the courage to let the past go and start again. I was scared and now I feel guilty, because maybe I had the chance to be happy with someone but everything is irrecoverable. I tried, but nothing. He doesn't want to be with someone insecure, who can blame him?"

"Oh my gosh, surely he'll understand!"

"No doctor, he won't, I'm sure!" I answered with sadness. I was resigned to the fact I had lost forever the opportunity that life gave me in that moment. "But anyway, it doesn't matter, there is a remedy to everything... or nearly everything!" I answered trying to avoid the subject.

"To conclude the string of negative events" I said with tears in my eyes, "in November my grandmother passed away."

"Your mother's mother? I had no idea!"

"Yes doctor, she had a stroke, the situation got worse. That's what happened. I miss her so much!"

The doctor was surprised, and answered: "Of course! Why didn't you come earlier to talk about it?"

"You are right, but I couldn't talk about it with anyone."

"Don't worry, I understand. In five months you have lost your family, your boyfriend and the grandma you grew up with! I understand you feel let down and totally lost. But now Paola, it's time to think about yourself a little bit, what do you think?" She answered with a motherly smile.

"Yes, ok, but how can I do it?" I asked, resigned.

"When you hit rock bottom, the only thing to do is to start again from yourself, there are no alternatives. Maybe you were not doing this for a while and life wanted to shake you suddenly. Now maybe, with three negative events on your back, you are realizing this."

I had never thought about it in this way before. "Are you telling me that everything comes down to this because I need to work on myself?"

"Well I can't give you a sure answer but probably yes.

Paola, you deserve to be happier than this, especially at your age. Look at you today, you look like an old rug. Don't you think it's time to take your life in your hands and enjoy what it gives you?"

That moment took my breath away. The doctor clearly explained that if I wanted happiness I had to go and take it, starting with myself.

"At this moment, believe me doctor, I don't even know where I am!"

"I know!" She answered me, as if she perfectly knew what to do.

"Listen, reflect on what we've talked about today, come here in a couple of days and let's create a plan together! In the meantime, think about what you would like to achieve in your life. Is there anything that makes you feel good?"

To skate! I immediately thought, but I didn't say it fearing it would have been too trivial.

"Think about it and you will see that you will obtain a lot more than you think now! Just do me a favor: start to write down ten positive features about yourself every evening for twenty-one days. I know you will struggle to find them now but don't give up! We will see each other the day after tomorrow at 2 o'clock, ok?"

"Ok doctor, thank you!" I answered, though slightly confused.

"You'll see that we'll put everything in place, I'm sure you will fly out of the nest!" She concluded with a huge smile.

I thanked her. That woman cleared more in one hour, than I had done alone in eight months. I realized that going to see her was the best decision I could have made at the time. While I was going down the stairs that led me to the main door, I was repeating to myself: "God bless you Doc!"

After that appointment, every appointment since then and every day since then, I cannot help but say that the doctor has become an essential point of reference for my personal, sentimental and sporting growth.

So, I needed to work on myself and use the little energy available to me. I was determined to rise back up and take the place that rightfully belonged to me in the world.

I arrived at the second appointment right on time. I couldn't wait as I really wanted to start this program and I was firmly convinced that it was the only thing I could do in that moment.

"Good morning Paola!" You look much better than the other day, you know?" The doctor greeted me with a big hug!

"Yes doctor I'm actually better. I cried a lot over the last few days but I think it was beneficial to let go."

"Sometimes it is necessary. I'm glad our meeting was helpful! Did you find ten positive features?"

"Actually, it was difficult. I tried, but I could only find seven!"

"It doesn't matter, go on. Repeat them initially, and you will see that others will come out, don't give up."

Giving up was the last thing I would have done, as I had only just started.

"So, did you think about what you wish to achieve? What is the thing that makes you feel good right now?"

"I know it may seem trivial, but what always made me feel good was to skate. Even in the difficult times, skating has always been my release. The skating rink is the place where I can express myself."

In the most difficult times it's Art that saves us.
Creativity is the safe port where we shelter whenever the inner sea is agitated.

41

"Perfect!" She said. Who knows what she had in mind, she always knew how to amaze me!

"What music are you using for your skating choreography?" She continued.

"*Lord of the Dance*. Do you know it?"

"Of course I do, it's the Irish one!"

"Exactly."

"Guess what? This year you will be the Queen of the Dance." She added with a big smile.

My face lit up. "You know doctor, I don't know why but I thought about the same thing when I chose it!"

"So it's a sign!" She firmly said. "Tell me, what competitions are you entering this year?"

"The same as usual, the most important one is the National Championship in July. This time they have separated male and females in my specialty, so even us women finally have a bit of hope to compete at a higher level."

"What would be the best competition you could participate in?"

Surprised by this question I answered with a half-smile.

"Well, the World Championship."

"Great! This year you will win the World Championship!"

I didn't burst out laughing, just to be polite. It's good to aim high but, even winning a World Championship medal seemed a bit of an exaggeration!

Maybe because she isn't part of the skating world she can't imagine what that means. Those were my thoughts...

I tried to answer in a nice way without offending her: "It seems like such an extraordinary thought but last November I came fourth in a competition that's not even a European Championship. I don't think it will be possible!"

"Believe it or not, you are right anyway," she answered with an aphorism from Henry Ford.

She had caught me off guard and I didn't know what to say.

"If you are really convinced about taking control of your life, you have to take risks! You have to aim high and have the courage to rise from the masses. Otherwise you will remain right where you are now."

Her words, sharp as blades, didn't leave me any way out. By now I had decided to take a leap of faith and I had nothing to lose.

"Ok doctor, let's suppose my main target is to win the World Championship," I resumed the conversation, without really believing in what I was saying, "How do I start?"

She gave me a huge smile and with a twinkle in her eyes she said: "Start today! To obtain a result, a real warrior needs first of all to believe in herself and trust her own capabilities! I think it's a good place to begin, that's why I let you start by asking you to locate your positive features."

In fact, my self-esteem in that moment was under my feet. She was right, the first step was to trust myself!

"Ok, apart from the ten features that I have to find every day, what else should I do?" I was frightened but curious to find out the answers.

"When you leave here, get yourself a gift, any gift, something you like that makes you feel special! Treat yourself as a princess. Remember Paola, it's the time to put yourself first. Stop being behind everything and everyone! You need to learn to love yourself, that's what you need to do!"

I already understood that I didn't love myself enough and the doctor highlighted the same thing. It was time to make up for it and get to work!

"All right doctor, I promise I will do my best! When will I see you again?"

"Paola, at the moment we need to work on the biggest part of this program. Let's meet again next week at the same time. All right?"

It seemed a bit soon for another appointment but I trusted her and agreed.

There are no limitations to the mind except
for those that we acknowledge.
Napoleon Hill

A Gift for Myself

I left the doctor's office in a whirlwind of conflicting emotions. On one side I was enthusiastic to start this program but on the other side I was scared to fly out of the nest. I was still let down, as much as I tried to be positive, I lived in continuous highs and lows during the day. I felt a strong sense of abandonment: three big losses within five months had brought me down to earth, but I had decided to get myself up and moving anyway.

The doctor suggested to buy myself a gift and I did. It seemed fun, but I really didn't know what to get. I wanted it to be significant. After several laps around the historic center of Genoa, I noticed a ring. It was silver and very plain. I immediately understood it was the right gift!

The ring is the symbol of union and, given the solitude of that period, I needed to be connected with the only person really important at the moment: myself. I went into the shop, I bought it and I wore it immediately. Simple, unique and made just for me! I was wandering around the city center and I didn't want to go back home. All of a sudden, as if dragged by a sixth sense, I went to a book shop and wandered on the ground floor where they had cookbooks and tourist guides. I wasn't satisfied, so I went on the next floor, where I found everything else, but nothing attracted me in that moment. Whilst I was going out, by the tills, a book with a dark red cover grabbed my attention. I went closer to it and I read the title: "The Secret." I took it in my hands and I turned it over. The cover talked about a "law of attraction," I opened the book to a random page and a quote from Joseph Campbell hit me:

If you follow your bliss, doors will open for you that wouldn't have opened for anyone else.

45

I immediately decided to buy it. That day took another turn. It seemed like something was moving inside of me.

The law of attraction says that "we attract exactly what we think" and our mindset influences events.

If you concentrate on obscure and negative thoughts, you will stay in that mood. If instead, when you take an action, you focus on positive thoughts and you have clear goals to reach, the law of attraction will help you to manifest what you want. Consciously or unconsciously, every second of our existence, we act like human magnets, sending thoughts and emotions, and attracting to us what we believe in. Not so much what we want or think we want!

At that moment I changed my mental attitude, or at least I tried to and, as a result, the things that began to happen were in line with my thoughts. I wanted to be reborn and I did nothing but meet situations and people who supported me in this venture. One morning, one of my patients, a lady in her sixties, who was attending psychology classes, pulled some papers for me out of her bag:

"I brought you some notes I took on a course, maybe they will interest you!"

"So kind of you! I will gladly read them, thank you!"

"I hope you will understand my handwriting, otherwise I can explain it to you. I also brought you this cartoon, always keep it in mind."

She placed in front of me a paper sheet with a little man drawn with the words "Always be a friend to yourself, because in times of need you are always nearby."

I was amazed! Another clear signal that I had to love myself! "Thank you so much, these notes are really perfect for me!"

Sometimes we meet people who, for a short time, enter our lives and they leave us with a very clear message about the direction we should take. They are like angels passing by and drawing out for us the way to go.

In the rehabilitation center, during the last month, my co-workers had improved significantly. Two colleagues had been hired who had been on the same degree course as me. Matteo, with whom I often used to joke and it was always pleasant to have a chat with, and Daniela, a woman older than me, who gave me a sense of peace. It was nice to spend time in her company and I began to realize that she knew so much. She always popped up with useful advice suited to the exact situation I was experiencing at that time. Daniela also attended a *Rolfing* course in Bologna, a very interesting physical therapy discipline that allows you to unblock the body tensions accumulated over time.

"You know, mind and body are the same thing, a person's body reflects what he lived," she explained to me. The topic was very interesting.

I said, "Yes I agree. Then if your mind and body are united, your emotional traumas also influence the body. Isn't that true?"

"Sure! Your body is nothing but the result of your past experiences. It talks and it tells you who you are. It never lies! Rolfing helps to keep you calm about these "traumas" and to find the correct posture and the mobility of the spine to move in the most fluid way for your body. It's very interesting, don't you think?"

"Yes of course! Dani, I fully agree with what you're saying. Actually, when I see a person, for the first time, I can understand roughly who I have in front of me. I think this happens because the body contains life experiences that are visible to me."

"Exactly, and your body now tells me you need help!" She replied with a smile. At this point we had a nice friendship developing between us. Daniela always had a sensible answer to my questions. In that stressful time, I was in fact suffering from pain in my lower back and one day, while I underwent a self-treatment, she said to me: "Paola, at the course, we were advised to test ten sessions of Rolfing on a person, I thought of you! Since you have back pain and you need a hand, do you want to be a guinea pig?"

"Dani, are you serious? I would be honored!"

"We can start right this week, straight after work, eat something together and then come to my practice which is right around the corner."

I was so surprised; another person was willing to help me out in that moment. Her treatments would go on to help me both physically and mentally.

I certainly had a few things to let go. "Dani, thank you for choosing me, I can't wait to get started!"

"It's a pleasure for me, you're a friend and I want to help you!" She concluded with a bright smile.

If you want to realize your dreams, you have to learn to know yourself.

INSTRUMENTS – VISUALIZATION AND BELIEFS

Visualization

The sessions with the doctor were proceeding regularly twice a month. She would always give me advice, make reason, comfort me emotionally and especially help me see life from another point of view. One day she said: "Well, Paola, we've analyzed your past, your family, your fears, all that has made you become the person you are today. We've seen that you need to feel good about yourself and put yourself first! You've understood that happiness is a choice and that to evolve, every now and then, you need to lose your balance. What matters, is finding a new equilibrium and always put yourself back at the helm of your own life. The time has now come to look towards the future, in the true sense of the word."

I couldn't imagine what training plan she had in mind for me, but I trusted her.

"Look towards the future? Could you explain yourself better, doctor?"

"You need to learn to visualize."

"Well, I already do, a little." I answered, almost disappointed by her statement.

"Very good, explain what you do."

"I visualize myself while I'm skating, while I perform my choreography and I imagine the music." I replied, slightly perplexed.

"That's not enough!" she interrupted me bluntly. "Your visualization is inadequate. You have to put something more into it, the fundamental ingredient is missing."

"What do you mean by that?" I asked curiously.

"Emotion. You need to enter into the visualization with all of yourself. It has to be you, while you are personally, really, living the event, as if it were happening in that precise moment! Enrich the situation with all the sensations, the smells and the tastes that you perceive in that moment. Remember that a visualization without emotions has no effect on your subconscious and, as a result, will never fulfill itself. If you really want to create a new neuronal pathway in your brain, you need to proceed with awareness, knowing that nothing can be overlooked and, when I say nothing, I mean that you must visualize even the facial expression you will have when you finish the competition! Remember, too, that the emotional part is what really moves the world. Between the rational and the emotional, emotional always wins."

This last affirmation wasn't clear to me, but I let it go. Sooner or later, I would understand. The part about the visualization, however, was crystal clear.

"In fact, I've never visualized like that. I'm curious to try it!"

"Let's start right now," she replied, "Let's go over there. We can start with five minutes of relaxation on the couch and then I'll guide you into the visualization. Today we'll visualize your perfect competition, the one that will make you win the World Championship!"

"All right, doctor, but what do you mean by the "perfect competition?" If I've never had a perfect competition, especially lately, how do I manage to visualize it?"

"Excellent question, Paola. It doesn't matter. Now it's a question of tapping into your most powerful creativity! Remember that anything, before happening, first "inhabited" someone's mind. I never said it would be easy. Quite the contrary. It's a form of training, just like physical training. Not everything will be successful right away, it's just a matter of trying and retrying until it happens automatically! In this, you're an expert, aren't you? Today is only lesson one! Begin by visualizing your perfect competition spiced with the joy, the love and the enthusiasm you want to feel. Are you ready?"

"Very well, I'll rely on your voice. Is it fine if I visualize the Italian Championship since it will be the one where I'll be selected for the World Championship?"

"Of course, Paola, that's very good. Your next goal will be the Italian Championship. When exactly will it be held?"

"Mid July."

"We've got two full months ahead of us! Promise me that you'll dedicate at least ten minutes every day on your own to visualizing. Don't worry if it's not easy at first. You just continue. It's very powerful work. In this way, you'll build a mental neuronal pathway which will activate itself when needed, that is, at the moment of the competition!"

Not everything that the doctor was saying was clear, to me. It seemed like pure magic. But something was inviting me to believe, to continue and especially to trust in her advice.

"But remember something very important! If you make a mistake during the visualization, and you will, just rewind the tape and visualize until you get it just as you want it. It's a training and you risk making a mistake but we don't want that. Let's go over there, I'll guide you!"

I was excited and curious. I could feel my heart thumping. I took a deep breath and, guided by the doctor's pleasant voice, I relaxed on the couch, ready to mentally build the perfect competition which would allow me to take off towards the World Championships! The doctor guided me into a state of complete relaxation and into the competition. Incredibly, I managed to visualize clearly and I entered my perfect competition. She then guided me onto the top step of the podium and I felt an intense emotion, the very same I felt as a little girl when I won my first competitions and raised the cup to the sky. I roused from the visualization with tears in my eyes exclaiming, "Doctor, this is fantastic!"

"I told you it was going to be a unique experience. I'm happy that you managed from the start to get inside to the maximum, with all of your emotional power! Now, you need to continue on your own, every day! Remember that visualizing just once won't get you anywhere."

I was so enthusiastic that I didn't hesitate in replying: "Of course, doctor, I'll do it every day, even a few times a day! I've understood the importance of foreseeing the future. I believe that in this way I'll even reduce pre-competition nerves!"

"Undoubtedly, that's how it will be. We'll see each other in two weeks and make sure to call me if you need to."

I thanked her with a hug. This woman had opened another window in my mind. I could feel the energy beginning to nourish my body like sap which supports, nurtures and sustains life. I couldn't wait to repeat the visualization; I was dazzled by it. The next morning, I decided to eat lunch outside after work to visualize by the seashore. The sound of the waves, the warm May sun, the salty sea smell, all brought me quickly to the state of calmness and tranquility of the day before. I tried to visualize my perfect competition but this time there were errors and inaccuracies and, mindful of the doctor's warning, I was afraid of making the mistake. I opened my eyes and my disappointment started to grow. Why had everything gone so perfectly the day before and now it seemed so difficult? Perhaps the doctor's guidance was missing? She has forewarned me that it wouldn't have been easy. However, I didn't throw in the towel. It came to mind that I could try visualizing to music. After all, you skate to the rhythm of music and music would help me to enter the competition better. Day after day, I tried and retried. When I visualized any mistake, I would go back in my mind and repeat the sequence. I didn't lose heart. I had understood that I could also do it while in motion which was a turning point. So I started visualizing while strolling on the beach. I would disconnect from the world and take refuge inside my bubble. I took on funny expressions and postures connected to my mental images but I didn't care what people would think of me. It was fun. As time passed, I was becoming more and more skillful and I could manage while running. Physical and mental training at the same time! The great thing about visualization is that you can do it anywhere and at any moment. During the sessions, the doctor guided me and helped me to better focus on my goal: winning the Italian Championship in order to qualify for the World Championship. Talking about it now it seems easy, but at the time I couldn't even manage to pronounce it. Nevertheless, I had faith and I continued.

Beliefs

The physical training was proceeding well. Daniela's treatments had made my body more supple and I could get into positions that I had previously given up on because of my rigidity. Everything seemed to make sense. But the first compulsory dance, the quickstep, was the biggest hurdle. I had already tried confronting it two years before and I hadn't managed to overcome it. I was convinced that I just wasn't cut out for a quick rhythm. I wasn't, however, getting off to a good start. I spoke with the doctor at our next session.

"Good, the first beliefs are starting to pop up, I was waiting for them!"

I was waiting for them? I repeated to myself. "What does that mean, doctor?"

"It means that each of us has a belief system; rules which tell you what is true and correct."

"Please explain yourself better."

"You see, Paola, from the moment you were born, you have had values drummed into you, beliefs that have made their way into your mind and your subconscious. The people who raised you: parents, grandparents, teachers, in addition to society, religion, the system in general, all launched messages which you have absorbed and they have transformed into rules which can obviously be either empowering or disempowering. I'll give you an example. If, since you were a little girl, everyone told you that you were capable and that everything you want to do in life, you will be a success at, this is an empowering belief, because for you this a rule and so, you'll do what has to be done to show yourself and others that it is true. If, however, for whatever reason, your rule was for example: "Whatever you do is bound to fail," you won't go very far and, what's more, you'll do all you have to in order to show yourself and others that you don't deserve the success! Whatever happens, you will give your maximum in order to confirm that this rule is true. Remember that your subconscious always wants to be right!"

I was shocked by this teaching, many things were much clearer and, almost incredulously, I answered:

"So, if I believe that beginning with a dance whose rhythm is as fast as the quickstep, just isn't for me, I'll do all I can to prove that this is so?"

"Exactly, Paola, and thank goodness this belief came out into the open!"

"Gosh!" I exclaimed, wide-eyed, "I need to understand what my other disempowering beliefs are!"

"Certainly, but in the meantime, let's straighten out this one."

"Right doctor, tell me how."

"Each time you try this dance, you have to repeat to yourself that you are cut out for it, that you are capable of doing the quickstep and that it's a perfect first dance for you! Is that clear?"

"Yes, ok. I just need to repeat it? And... if I don't really believe it?"

She burst out laughing: "Remove the just, because the brain functions on habits and repetitions, that's why repeating things works, and how! It's clear that you don't believe, otherwise your belief would already have disappeared, do you understand what I mean?"

"Yes, Doc, in fact, you're perfectly right! So: I mentally repeat until I manage to substitute the disempowering belief, right?"

"Exactly! And when you start believing in it, it means your job is well under way. Remember that beliefs are self-fulfilling prophecies. You'll see how important they can be in your life."

Once again, the doctor had hit the mark. Thinking about it, I understood why I had boycotted myself all my life and how many times I had lost competitions because of my limiting beliefs. This also frightened me a bit. Who knew how many other beliefs were inside of me without my even realizing it? I sighed and decided to start working on the belief that had just emerged. If others were going to pop up, now I had an instrument to confront them with.

95% of the beliefs of we have stored in our minds are nothing but lies and we suffer because we believe all these are true.

Don Miguel Ruiz

Italian Championships 2009

It was strange, although I was still going through moments of sadness, I felt a new energy was flowing through my body. As if, in addition to the fog in front of me, there was a ray of sunshine and heat; a delicate and magical protection that enveloped my mind, my body and my life. Many people had come to help me take the next step. For the first time perhaps, I felt at the helm of my life. I was ready to get back into the game with a different mentality. The sessions with Daniela lifted me, and every time I was leaving the practice in the evening or in the following days, I was always crying. Probably I was letting go of different emotions.

I also remember that for a week I hadn't worn my skates because they were being repaired and, when I put them back on, I couldn't stand up like before! It seemed like a clear sign that my body was acquiring new habits.

If you want to take a step forward you need to lose
your balance for a moment.
Massimo Gramellini

In the last year the emotional earthquake had made me continuously lose my balance. I had fallen over and over again, but every time I got up stronger. I had grown up and when I looked back I did not recognize myself anymore. Nothing had been easy, and from this lesson I understood that the people around us are more than fundamental in our life, but if we are not the first to take control, we will drift, probably onto a beach that isn't even ours. This time I decided to take up the reins of my life and what I wanted to achieve was clear in my mind. I had trained physically and mentally for the first time in my life. I meditated, I did breathing exercises, recharged myself in nature, visualized every day my perfect competition and my goal. I was preparing my field, I was sowing, watering and giving light, hoping to gather new flowers and fruits as soon as possible. It was almost time for the Italian Championships and that year they took place in Sardinia, in the province of Cagliari. Before leaving, I went to the doctor to receive her "blessing."

"Dear Paola, this is the moment of your personal revenge," She told me. "I have accompanied you so far, and I will always be there, but now it's your turn, you've prepared everything like a warrior, with determination, constancy and clarity of intent. Now you're ready to face the battle. Do it with love and courage, bring your light to the rink and fly lightly like a butterfly."

Taking these words with me, I left for the championship four days before the competition.

Coming a few days early to try out the rink has always been essential to me but, on that occasion, I was strangely quiet, with a different feeling compared to the previous competitions.

I had never stopped training mentally, the doctor had suggested that I see myself with butterfly wings, in flight, colorful and transformed. The training went well. I remember that the day before leaving I spent the afternoon at the beach, in total carelessness, visualizing my perfect competition. The fateful day had come, the adrenaline was starting to flow and I was a bit anxious because, due to a strong wind and a change in climate, the rink had become extremely slippery. It was difficult to stand up, even with softer wheels. Many athletes fell and you could feel the panic in the air. That was the situation, you just had to adapt and have confidence in your abilities.

The final ten seconds before entering the rink, are essential to my story. I turned to my mother with me in that moment as my trainer: "Please, mom, shake me!" With her eyes wide, in a moment she became serious, and with a steady gaze, she replied: "Paola, do not be stupid, go out on the rink convinced of your abilities, I want to see you as gritty as when you were little... Give all of you, go on and have fun!" She grabbed my arm and with her eyes on mine she added, "How is the lion doing?"

I smiled at her and felt the roughness inside me that she helped me to find each time. It was a sentence that she repeated to me as a child, when I began my first competitions. I entered the rink with a pat on the bottom and forgot everything.

I so wanted the first track of the quickstep to be assigned to me because, among all the possibilities, it was the most suitable, and even if it wasn't up to me, magically it started to play. Amazed and excited, I danced the dreaded quickstep. It went really well! Despite being among the first to perform, I did not want to lose concentration: I still had to face the second dance, a waltz. Keep calm. After having dealt with the quickstep I felt completely free, and, precisely for this reason, I faced the rest of the competition with serenity. I was satisfied. For the first time I was on second position half way through the competition and I was more determined than ever.

I remember my mom telling me after the compulsory dances: "Paola, I don't want to disappoint you, but get ready because tomorrow they will do everything they can to get you off that podium!" With a force coming from my chest, I replied: "No mom, not this time, I want to believe I'm going to win it until the end!" She looked at me and did not answer. I think she only said it to prepare me for the worst. But this time I was ready, I wanted to pursue my goal with all my strength.

The next day the final competition was waiting for me, the rink was even more slippery and nothing could be done to change the situation. I tried not to think about it, I just wanted to perform with all the joy that I had put into the program. I skated enthusiastically, with an energy I had never experienced before, light as a butterfly! The score was good; I was really satisfied with my performance. I didn't know the ranking yet, I only realized it when my mom, with tears in her eyes, ran to me and with a big hug told me: "Paola you won, you did it!" I could not believe it; my heart was beating so fast and I did not understand if it was a dream or reality! "I'm sure Nan had helped from up there!" Mom added with a broken voice. I burst into tears. It was true, she loved me and skating and she was certainly there with us. Since that day, she has always been my guardian angel and she has accompanied and protected me in every moment. I climbed on the top step of the podium a bit shyly, I couldn't quite believe it. To hear the Italian national anthem, which after many years, was playing for me again, was a unique experience, something that still dampens my eyes.

If you believe it, you can realize it.
Zig Ziglar

The Pre-World Championships

The first thing I did after the victory was to go to the doctor with a bouquet of flowers.

"Congratulations Paola, what a joy to see you so bright! I'm really happy for you, you did so well! Objective completed! I knew you could do it."

"I'm so enthused, I can't even comprehend what is happening to me, and do you understand that I'm going to the World Championship?"

"I know, that's what you wanted, right? So tell me, when will it be?"

"In the middle of November in Germany, I can't wait! When do we start the mental preparation? Do you know how powerful it was? I swear some people came to me and told me: you were as light as a butterfly on the rink!"

"Of course I believe in you my dear, these are very powerful techniques, and you will see that they will be extremely useful in your life."

"I know, I'm so curious, I read a lot about it and I want to learn more and more, thank you so much doctor, really!"

"It's a pleasure, and you deserve all of this, now enjoy a bit of vacation and we will soon start back for the World goal."

In the meantime, I received a call from Bologna. I had passed the audition to enter a prestigious musical school. I couldn't believe it! A passion for drama had always been part of me, as well as dancing and learning to sing. I had auditioned mostly just for fun, but I was selected! I thought seriously about moving to Bologna to start a new career but then, there was the World Championship that I did not want to give up at the same time. I let go of the opportunity but I was still happy and amazed that it had materialized all together.

I spent about ten days in Spain with a couple of friends and a few days in the mountains, where I started my training off of skates. I was happy to be selected for the competition even if, after all, a little voice inside me made me feel I didn't deserve it.

60

Sometimes we struggle to receive the positive things that life gives us because, after all, it's a change and that scares us. It's a feeling that I personally meet often and with whom I have to deal with all the time. I was unaware of this grey area, and my subconscious was probably scared of a new life that could really work.

On September 14th, a rainy day, I went to training alone. That day my mother told me: "Paola avoid going on the rink today. Nothing is going to happen if you take a day off! You are training well, at most you can workout off of skates a bit."

Skip a training session? Not at all. When I got on the rink, I dried it and started training with the music in my earphones. At one point I stopped for a moment to drink. An image appeared clearly in my mind: a berry on the ground and a child that had broken her arm here a few months earlier.

I felt a sense of anguish in my chest and though: I'm going to do one last lap and then take off my skates. Just as I was doing that last lap, one berry on the ground blocked my wheels and, without even realizing it, I found myself on the floor with a huge pain in my right elbow! I was shocked: the vision of a few minutes before had materialized! Why did I not listen to myself? I immediately called my mom who rushed to the rink and took me to the hospital.

There was no fracture from the scans. As a precaution, however, they put me in a cast and told me to keep that protection for a week. They recommended a CT scan if I had pain. I thought that after all that I was pretty lucky! Only a week of rest was not so bad. The day after the pain persisted, and again the day after; I couldn't even press the elevator button and I couldn't move my elbow at all. So I decided to go for the CT. The following morning at 7:30 AM, the telephone rang: "Miss Fraschini, we have the report: your elbow shows a fracture at the epicondyle, you need to come back to the hospital as soon as possible."

I felt myself dying inside. I had never suffered a fracture before. I woke up my brother who took me to the hospital and they casted me one more time for another three weeks. I was in pieces. Some doctors said that I would not be able to recover in time and this certainly didn't help my morale. Why did it happen at that moment with the championship at the door? I couldn't find a reason, I didn't have peace and I couldn't sleep. I was in a state of perpetual agitation where everything seemed to crumble to dust in the most beautiful moments. The doctor as usual, gave me a big hand.

"Paola this is a test! Life sometimes puts obstacles in your way just to see if you're ready to make a leap in quality. You have to face this moment as a warrior and you are a warrior. Be faithful and everything will go well. You'll be able to compete and win, I promise. Let's do our battle plan today."

Her words were like light that warmed my heart. I didn't want to give up. I wanted to at least try.

"Okay doctor, I want to trust you but with an elbow in this condition, I can't even run! The most I can do is some training off of skates..."

"But your winning card is mental training, now more than ever!" She interrupted me.

For the Italian Championship I used a lot of visualization indeed. I imagined my performance several times, exactly as I wanted it to be, and if it had already worked, why it couldn't also happen for the World Championship?

"Paola, take the time to visualize your perfect competition every day, as you have already done, but this time

I'll ask you one more thing. I want you to visualize the award ceremony, I want you to see yourself up there on the rooftop of the world, because that's where you deserve to be my dear."

I sighed and accepted the new challenge. "All right doctor, I have nothing to lose. In fact, I can do nothing but learn new things from this experience. I want to try and believe it all the way."

"Well done Paola, that's the way I want you to be! Remember that there is nothing more powerful than your will. If you want you can really do it, I'm sure you're able to deal with this situation at the best of your abilities. I will guide you. If there's anything you may need, you know I'll always be here."

"I am grateful doctor; I promise I will do my best."

That's how I decided to start my alternative training program. Every morning I got up and I walked along the seafront listening to the music of my competition routine and skating in my mind. I was into the part, I corrected what was wrong, and I lived the competition at least thirty times, every day. I walked and I visualized. I put in all the most beautiful emotions that I knew and I saw myself on the highest step of the podium. In the evening I used to go to the rink to do exercises off of skates. I spent a month like this, with so many highs and lows, moments of hope alternated with some of frustration, but I kept going.

In the meantime, I continued teaching skating and Physio-Pilates and this helped me to distract myself. I felt that slowly my elbow was healing and, after a month, it was finally time to remove the cast. Once free however, my elbow was not the same anymore. I was not able to move my arm and I felt tremendously weak. I immediately started the rehabilitation and, after two days, the training as well. I was afraid of falling and getting hurt again and it wasn't easy to recover the damaged part.

I had three weeks to go before the competition, not many to train physically, but I did my best to make the most out of them. In addition to mental training I started physical training on the Alassio rink, not being able to count on Genoa. This was the best rink, more suitable, but required an hour and a half by car to get there and the same to come back. Most of the time my brother took me there, because my mom worked in a store in the morning and, when nobody could, I used to go alone. In the afternoon instead she trained me in Genoa. She used to say that everything was going alright and I was ready. At that moment I was very fragile and her affirmations were indispensable. It seemed like nothing was easy: my anxiety was growing, I used to sleep very little, the psychological tiredness was striking, the skates were hurting my feet and ankles because I hadn't worn them for a month. It all seemed insurmountable.

Fortunately, I received a lot of support from many people, and the doctor continued to repeat: "Have faith Paola. The elbow represents the change of direction; I know that it scares you. The universe is putting you under trial to see if you are able to receive what you will be given later. It will be a hundred times bigger and more incredible than what you're going through right now. Everyone is on your side to support you, everything will be fine!"

Begin by doing what is necessary, then what is possible.
And suddenly you will be surprised that you can do the impossible.
Saint Francis

World Championships 2009

The date of the World Championship was approaching; it was time to leave. Whatever the outcome was, for me it was already a success just to participate. After all, I had to experience it at least once.

When there is a destination, even the desert becomes a road.
Tibetan Proverb

I remember the trip, during the night, between thoughts and emotions. Everyone was sleeping, except for me. Only the noise of the cars through the windows was breaking the complete silence. That trip represented a personal challenge, I would need to get involved in a completely new way. I knew I was not physically strong, but I had to compete and do my best. A whole life dedicated to skating for the world's dream. Now I was there, one step away from all of it. Nobody knew about my fractured elbow, I preferred not to reveal that I couldn't train for a month.

I arrived in Freiburg on Sunday morning; the first competition was on Wednesday and the final on Thursday. Two days were the official trial period in which I could work the wheels so that they were suitable for the surface, set the drawings of the dances and adapt to the slippery and huge rink compared to what I was used to.

The rink in Genoa measures more or less 8,611 square feet and the competitions normally take place on an area of over 10,760 square feet: I was a goldfish thrown offshore. The trials went well but I was struggling to control my anxiety. The morning of the competition my brother and some friends had joined me and I felt their support. I counted a lot on their presence and having my mom as a coach meant being backed up every single moment. Everything was ready for the fateful first dance, the quickstep.

I entered with a smile and with the joy of being able to skate, to be there, despite everything. It went very well! Exiting the rink, I hugged my mother whispering in her ear: "Wonderful! I had fun!" I was in first position but I tried to keep calm. I had broken the ice and I was safer on the second dance, the waltz. A small slide, however, threw me into the third position. My morale went down a bit but fortunately we were only halfway through the competition. There was everything still to play for.

The next day was the free dance, my winning weapon, choreographed the year before at the time when my life apparently went to pieces. Skating and distracting myself with something creative was my only source of peace. I had chosen the music of Lord of the Dance for the intense emotion that they had given to me. Full of energy and hope, people told me that that year I would become the "Queen of the Dance" as the doctor underlined.

When I arrived in Freiburg, the city was carpeted with billboards of the Irish company coming soon and the title *Lord of the Dance* stood out in large letters. It seemed like a great sign and it wasn't the only one... During that week I heard several times that the universe was on my side and that it wanted to reward me for my determination and for having overcome my small and big battles. I received messages of encouragement from friends and people from all over the world. But the most significant one was from my physical therapist, Dr. Fusco: "What you have to do tomorrow is disconnect the mind from the body." I hadn't figured out what he meant by that message, but I thanked him and didn't really pay any attention to it. The doctor wrote to me: "Keep on visualizing yourself on the top of that podium!" The day of the finals had come and I didn't stop seeing myself up there, despite everything that had happened.

That night I had unexpectedly slept very well and I was regenerated! A little nervous, of course, but ready, and eager to face the last challenge.

When I shut the door of my room to go to the skating rink, I realized I had forgotten Patty, the soft toy lucky charm that my grandmother had sewn for me for my first competition, which I am very fond of. I went back, picked Patty up from the bed and my eye fell on the back of the book that I had left on the bedside table.

The Warrior of Light believes in miracles, and because he believes, miracles begin to happen.
Paulo Coelho

That sentence surprised me so much that it almost frightened me. I had never really considered it before that moment. I took a breath and ran to the rink. I entered the arena visibly emotional and got ready for the competition quickly. I felt the need for a long warm up, I could not stand still. The official warm up went very well but the tension that had accumulated over the months peaked five minutes before entering the rink and I burst into tears. I couldn't contain myself, I knew, however, that it was an outlet. It freed my mind from so many worries and brought me back to the present. My mother was with me: "Paola it's your time, you can't give up now, think of all you've been through, you've prepared the free dance as you like and now it's your moment. Go for it and have fun!"

I entered with a smile, an emotion that came from my heart and expanded throughout my body. The music started and after the first three steps I realized that my left skate was loose... I began to panic! Throughout the whole choreography I kept repeating to myself: "And now what can I do? Do I stop? If I stop, I throw everything away! How is that possible? Yet another misfortune! Breathe! Ok I try to move on. Now I'm on the right, and now left."

My rational mind feared for what was happening, but the non-rational part was activated. The words of my physical therapist were beginning to come true: I had literally disconnected my body from my mind. I arrived at the end of the choreography without even realizing it, as if I'd been on autopilot. I wasn't out of breath and in a flash I realized that it had actually gone well. Everything I had visualized mentally for months had manifested itself. Once I finished the program, I started to jump and scream for joy, I could not believe my eyes! The score was great, the display marked Place 1, but I didn't understand if it was the total score or the partial one, I had to wait for the end of the competition to find out.

In the meantime, I was in another dimension, as if I had already lived that situation beforehand, my mind and my body were travelling through a whirlwind of indescribable sensation. I only realized I had won when everyone came up to congratulate and hug me. The ranking on the big screen was up, it was all true... I was the World Champion!

The miracle had really happened, everything had been put in place for me to get that result. It was a big effort, nothing had gone the right way from the beginning, but I had continued to believe in it, to overcome every obstacle. Moreover, everything spoke to me: the billboards, the book, the message of the physical therapist... Even the loose skate had allowed me to disconnect my rational mind and, as if that wasn't enough, I won the World Championship on November 19th, 2009. The 19th of July 2009 I had won the Italian Championship and the 19th was also the day of the birth of my grandmother, who passed away exactly one year before. She cared so much about me and my competitions. I looked at myself in the mirror and I saw another me. I had won a long and difficult battle and a gold medal around my neck said it clearly: it was my rebirth. I had managed to climb the chasm, drawing on all of my resources, dreaming big and overcoming the trials that life put in front of me. It was as if they had screamed at me: "Wake up! There's a lot more than you think!" Everything that happened to me was so incredible, I was almost afraid to be taken for crazy when telling people about it.

But I couldn't remain indifferent, I had to understand more. So I started to dedicate myself to research, study, experiments, to deeply understand what I had just started to discover. In that moment I realized that we are much more powerful than what we believe we are, that we must learn to get to know ourselves and trust our abilities and that the universe always wants the best for our personal evolution.

Greatness really exists in each one of us. Show your values.
Stop doing everything to please others.
Stop realizing the dreams of others. Take your life in your hands
and start to fly towards your realization.

Chapter 4
2010 Handling Fears

I had won the World Championship with less than three weeks of physical training and months of mental training. I had accessed a dimension that I couldn't even imagine had existed.

It was obvious that there was much more behind the curtain of common life for me, and I was becoming aware of it.

I felt deeply responsible for the interior richness that I had experienced. After the dive, it was time to explore that world. I had a feeling that I was miraculous, like when you win a game for the first time and you think it is just beginner's luck. Was it really just luck? The question resounded in my mind but looking at my gold medal I was repeating to myself that it wasn't just magic because the results were real. I was no longer identifying myself with the person I was just nine months before. I had grown up, or rather, evolved. In one year I had taken giant steps. I had decided that I deserved much more, that I had to start from within myself and, above all, I had started to give a clear direction to my life. I had fought my personal battles, believing and overcoming obstacles and crises.

What a great life lesson! The difficulties came to test me and see if I was really ready to welcome what happened to me. In some moments I wanted to give everything up, I admit, but I learned to always be stronger and more aware.

That experience showed me that I had always owned that strength within me, but before I didn't know how to express it.

In the following years, the biggest challenge was to keep the title of World Champion. No competition was ever a foregone conclusion but I always succeeded. I studied and applied the techniques I had learned with commitment and constancy giving more and more value to mental preparation. The doctor continued to follow me step by step in the competitions and in my daily life. She always knew exactly what I needed. She gave me practical tools to work on for myself and my competitions.

I was hungry to know more, so I decided to attend a sports psychology master's degree program in Milan. I was reading a lot of books and constantly informing myself.

In those years I also met Max Gentile, who was very important for my growth. With him I did a two year course and individual sessions that helped me to rediscover my spiritual side and, above all, to work towards the direction that I wanted my life to go in.

I am infinitely grateful to everyone who has supported me and taught me so much on the path towards my self-realization.

Going on, I needed even more intense mental support, as well as physical training. In fact, in winning the title every year, the expectations grow, and consequently the responsibility. But I understood that I could actively direct my life instead of passively undergoing the circumstances that it threw at me. I have always lived the competitions like they were personal battles: I had to do a deep dive into myself and pull out resources that I didn't even imagine that I had. The competitions brought me to a place where I had to look straight at my true essence, I couldn't hide, I had to face my limits, my fears and my obstacles. I had to learn to break through the inner walls that hadn't allowed me to fly out of the nest.

In those years I eliminated the veils that imprisoned my soul and I slowly tried to spread my wings. It's a process that will continue forever in my life, but the competitions led me to get closer to myself.

During the World Championships I was offered to skate in a dance couple with Marco Brogi, an athlete from Rome. He was looking for a new partner to continue his career with. I was really excited about the opportunity and even my mom supported me in full: "Paola it's your time now, you've fought so much for this, go for it!" She was right, I couldn't stop just when a new door had opened. I knew it wouldn't be easy because of the distance, but I immediately went to Rome for a trial day. We were great on the rink together, there was a good initial chemistry, but how could we organize the Genoa-Rome training? I would have to meet him in Rome because the choreographies were prepared there, but I was willing to try this new experience. I wanted to invest in myself, in my skating. Being an athlete was at the forefront of my mind. It would be an intense 2010: I wanted to continue with Solo Dance as well as competing in pairs.

My enthusiasm was high, higher than any sacrifice I had to make to support travel to Rome every four days, fitting in work, individual training, mental preparation and also the commitment I had as a volunteer head scout. I was happy when the trains were on time or when I found a cheap flight that allowed me to be there within a couple of hours. I worked as a physical therapist and trainer. Basically I have always worked hard to support the costs of skating, but it was fine that way. In this sport, even if done at professional level, nothing is given as a gift, it is done exclusively for passion.

In 2010 I wanted to confirm myself in Solo Dance and get the best in pairs. Psychologically, confirming yourself involves a lot of mental stress. You're always wondering if you are good enough.

So, I had to prepare an adequate action plan. Even in this case, my doctor helped and followed me from start to finish evaluating each indecision, blockage or fear. The advice that particularly helped me was this: "Paola, to continue to achieve goals in life you must learn to put your past behind you, but to treasure it."

"Doctor, what should I do in practice?"

"You must look at your past as something precious from which you have learned important lessons to grow, but you can't remain anchored to it."

It is necessary to find the courage to turn the page and turn it by looking at the future while living in the present.

"Only in this way will you be really focused on your life's true direction. With the competitions you have to do exactly the same. 2009 has taught you a lot and has paid off your efforts with so much satisfaction. That will remain forever in your heart, but if in your mind you are just looking at the past successes you won't be able to fully enjoy what the future can bring you. Do you follow me?"

"Yes, doctor, it's clear, but how can I treasure these teachings so that they can stay with me forever?"

INSTRUMENTS: TRAINING DIARY

"There is a very powerful instrument called writing: spoken words fly away, written words remain." She said smiling.

"Write down what you have learned during this year. In this way you will fix in your mind the key concepts that have brought you here and you won't forget them anymore. Buy a notebook where, from now on, you will write down what you have learned and are learning. Start with the things that happened to you last year. Read them again, take a deep breath and then turn the page. On a blank page write today's date and start your training diary where you will write something every day. It's not necessary to dwell, sometimes only a couple of words or a phrase are enough. Put black on white and this will help you to maintain and increase mental clarity. Also, even visually, to write on a white and empty page, will make you feel more motivated. It will be a tool that will allow you to keep track of your life and give a name to your thoughts, emotions and worries."

It seemed simple and brilliant. In my past I had kept a diary but I had not been consistent, however, writing my thoughts has always given me massive help. Indeed, I often feel the physical need of seeing with my own eyes what the mind tells me and then everything becomes clearer.

"So I write in the diary a kind of story about what happened to me last year, right? And how does that work for the training?"

75

"Paola I don't want to give you too many rules. Don't think too much. Look for your personal approach, you can make it more schematic or more fictional and highlight the important lessons. You can do the same for your next training regime. Use your imagination and I'm sure you will find your own way to express yourself."

This answer didn't satisfy me but I understood that she wanted to help me with my freedom of expression. There are those who are more visual, who need graphics, who draw and who need words. I already knew that my method consisted of writing and highlighting the most important parts.

"Okay doctor, I'll start tomorrow. It really seems like a useful tool."

"It is, you will see how important it will be for your personal and sporting growth. Start with this and next time you come, bring it here with you."

I thanked her and started to use the diary that very day. I wrote about everything that happened in 2009 and this gave me incredible strength to face the subsequent obstacles.

I repeated to myself: "If I did it under those conditions, I can do it again and even better!"

The doctor was right, it was a way to treasure what I had learned and it gave me necessary strength to move forward with more decisiveness, enthusiasm and courage. I began to write constantly in the diary and it turned out to be extremely helpful.

Every day, at the end of training, I spent five minutes to initially pin down what was going well, then what I could improve on, the corrections of the coach, and finally I gave it a score from 0 to 10.

Eventually, I left room for some notes mainly dedicated to emotions, feelings, concerns and strengths. It was very simple, essential and fast but it allowed me to go to the next training session with clearer ideas. It's a tool that I recommend to everyone.

Italian Championships 2010

I spent weeks going between Genoa and Rome. My life was quite demanding and tiring but also so fulfilling. During my travels I read a lot, I studied and I listened to music that inspired me to create new choreographies. The training for pairs proceeded well and the new programs rewarded me although I still didn't know which music to choose for my singles choreography. I wanted to use the soundtrack of the film *The Fabulous World of Amelie* by Yann Tiersen. I remember I tried to put together the tracks but the result didn't satisfy me and I lost a lot of time as I couldn't save the music file. I took this as a sign that I shouldn't have chosen them. One day I was casually listening to music on YouTube when a sponsorship of *Nine*, the new musical dedicated to Fellini, came up. I was immediately captured. I went to look for the soundtrack and I fell in love with it. It was perfect! I wanted to dance to it and it also happened to be a tribute to my nation. So, I decided to put together *Cinema Italiano* by Kate Hudson and *Be italian* by Fergie. In just half an hour I created my track perfectly. Sometimes we just need to wait and when the right thing comes, everything moves smoothly and without complications. And, anyway, even when situations do not flow immediately, it is important to learn to listen to your own body, whether these are crucial choices for life or related just to a moment. Before acting, take time, breathe with your eyes closed, and see what you physically feel in front of the choice you have to make.

Going with what you feel intuitively is authentic and less able to be disrupted by the mind.

The next day I went to the rink early to put together the new choreography, my ideas took shape easily in my inspired mind and became movements. In preparation for the Italian Championships, I continued my visualization program, like the previous year, and I used the training diary. Sometimes it was a real outlet for the excess of my thoughts. The visualization helped me to keep the mental focus on my target.

Despite the little time available, I dedicated part of it to walking, breathing, listening to the music, and entering a flow where everything was running smoothly together and in which I felt connected to myself and the universe. These were precious moments before the competition that always held the key to calming me down and putting me back in touch with the deepest part of myself.

But I was also very tired and under pressure because of the many trips during those months and, a week before my Solo Dance Championship, I had an acute inflammation of the left Achilles tendon. I couldn't even point my toes! It was impossible to push, especially when I went backwards on the skates. I had to find a solution if I wanted to compete. I took the broken skates I had from the year before, I inserted a rise below the heel and one below the toe, between the boot and the plate, in order to level the heights of both of them. My balance was totally different and there were only five days left to the Italian Championships.

"Why do I sabotage myself like this? Why there is always something before the competition that goes wrong?" I asked my doctor.

"Well it's your unconscious who wants to protect you!"

"Protect me?" I asked, surprised.

78

"I know it sounds strange but your unconscious is the layer that covers your soul. The unconscious is afraid, the soul is not. Fear can be a friend and an enemy. It can stop you so much that you can no longer go on, but it can also save you from dangerous situations. You must learn to befriend your unconscious. You are afraid to compete because you don't know how it will go. You're afraid of not being able to win your title, you're afraid to fail. It will always be like this unless you talk and reassure yourself. You have the opportunity to grow through this competition and become aware of your mental blocks. Remember that awareness is the first step to healing. We only have a few days now, but for the World Championship we will work more deeply. Now what you need to do is enter inside of yourself through meditation, talk with your unconscious, reassure and recharge yourself with positive energy. I can guide you in this, let's go to the other room, lay down, and you can get in contact with the deepest parts of yourself."

When a change enters our lives, no matter how positive it may be, it scares us, and our unconscious tries to protect us, keep us safe in all ways, and sometimes stop us.
Injuries are an example of this. Learn to reassure the unconscious by talking to it and listening to it in the right way, it's a fundamental step to not slow down our natural evolution.

That was how she guided me in one of the most beautiful meditations I've ever done in my life. I was able to go deep into and calm down the part of myself that was so worried. I finished the visualization gaining strength from the universe, from the galaxy, from the stars, feeling one with the creation. I opened my eyes and I finally saw the competition with a whole new point of view. I had to compete with the immense source of energy I'd just received.

79

I felt I had the strength to do my best, despite everything that had happened.

"Paola, after all, you like challenges! When you have to fight you always give your best. This is further proof, accept it and prepare for your next personal battle. I'm sure you will win."

As always, the doctor had charged me with an extraordinary energy. That year the Italian Championships were held in Calenzano, in the province of Florence. The heat was suffocating. The skating rink environment was, as always, slightly tense. I had too many eyes on me and the feeling of being continuously judged wouldn't leave.

I felt a sense of unease. My trials were mediocre and the rink was big and very slippery. I was nervous and, although the first part of the competition went quite well, it was not how I wanted it to be. I had earned the second position. I felt boiling emotions and was not satisfied because I hadn't given my best. A voice inside of me said: "This is not the right way of competing, it's not the way to win, I need to wake up!"

Before the free dance, my mother repeated to me her concept, understanding my state of mind: "Paola you don't go anywhere with the fear that stops you! Release all bridles that keep you tied down and let yourself go until the end... Risk it! You have nothing to lose!" She was right, I had to give all of myself if I wanted to gain a position and end as the winner.

During the free dance warm up a raging energy invaded me. I felt a fire coming from my heart, it freed me from all the chains that held me imprisoned. "Stop pretending, it's time to act!" I told myself. I entered the rink as number 19, the number of my grandmother. It was a sign that, again, she was with me. I didn't think of anything, just dancing and making sure that the music came through me and turned into emotions. It went very well, I finished the program and, I don't know where it came from, but I exclaimed: "This is me!" The score was high, the highest of all and I won a new Italian Championship! Despite my unconscious doing everything to put obstacles between the wheels I was able to overcome myself another time.

It helped me to understand that the year before it wasn't only fortune. I was mentally and physically present and I could aim high again.

2010 World Championships

I spent the summer training. In September the European Championships for couples with Marco would be held in Spain.

It went very well and we won the title. Despite the weight of the never ending journeys, the training sessions in Rome had allowed me to grow a lot technically and after our first year together we were satisfied.

From 2010 to 2014, even though they were very different, the years were marked above all by a word and a goal: To Reconfirm. Whenever there was a new challenge, a conquest or a lesson to learn, I had to be strong mentally and continue to invest in my personal growth.

In 2010, the World Championships would have been at the beginning of December in Portugal. Considering that I had concluded the Italian Championships at the end of July, the time between the two competitions was really long. That wait put me in a state of anxiety. On one side, I wanted to compete right away to take away my doubts and keep the motivation that I'd developed. On the other hand, I had to learn to wait and above all, to manage my fears.

When you're on the rink alone trying to regain the world title, you must find confidence every time. You must become stronger and stronger so that nothing can dismantle you. Fears come to the surface when we have to face challenges. The competitions have always put me in front of life's mirror, sometimes showing me some dark shadows. They stripped me of all the fake certainties I'd had and made me take a journey inside of myself to identify new positive and productive resources to use each time.

I had to face the second World Championship, maybe the hardest. The fear of not making it, of not getting to the same heights, to make mistakes and fail, pressed me hard.

My doctor told me: "As we just said before the Italian Championship, fear in itself is an energy that can be positive or negative, it depends how we react to it. Think about it, fear protects us from so many dangers, if you didn't have it you would be completely reckless! Try to channel your fear in the right direction; turn it into positive energy, into a challenge. Among the most common fears, with which we must often deal, there is that of failure, judgment, abandonment and of success..."

At that point I interrupted her: "No, wait a minute doctor why should we be afraid of success?"

She smiled as if she expected my question: "We fear what we don't know. Now answer this question: What does it mean to you to succeed?"

I reflected for a moment and then I said: "For me it means to be successful in something: work, sports, relationships.... Perhaps more than just having success, rather being a successful person: someone who achieves her goals, grows, evolves and wishes to share these successes with others."

"I really like your answer, but then, I ask you, why

should we be intimidated? It looks like a good and noble thing!"

I thought for a moment and answered back: "I'm afraid to lose the people who are close to me, I'm afraid to lose their affection. If I raise myself to a higher level and others are further down, there will be no more connection and I'm afraid of being alone. Perhaps success could bring me to solitude."

The doctor's face became suddenly sad. "I understand what you're saying, but the people who really love you, look at your success as an example to follow or as a guide to be inspired by, and they will be with you forever. On the contrary, people envious of your success do not deserve your attention and so it is better to lose them. Remember that true friends are those that are there above all in moments of joy, because it is easier to console those in difficulty rather than enjoy the success of others. In front of you they will feel frustrated because they didn't have the audacity, the strength and the patience to get involved... Because all of this is scary."

The doctor understood perfectly what was going on in my head and added:

"Remember that to overcome our fears we have to get outside of our comfort zone, that psychological space in which we feel safe because it's what we know best. That space in which everything that happens is familiar and where we feel protected. Making that jump provokes anxiety, stress and fear and nobody likes to feel under pressure. Therefore, the cowardly will remain in their enclosure for life, they will be safe but they will never evolve. On the contrary, those who choose to slowly take a step forward and feel the unknown ground will evolve, change and overcome themselves. It's not easy because it means going deep within yourself and coming to terms with what you have inside but, you see, there are no shortcuts. If you want to evolve it is from there that you have to pass through, the life is yours, and the choice of who you want to be is yours."

"I want to be a successful person, I'm ready to face my fears at all costs and I want to be a good example for others!" I answered spontaneously.

The doctor, with a motherly look, told me:

"You are on the correct path and I have understood that in front of difficulties you don't stop, you are a warrior. Keep going and remember to trust yourself and the universe. You will see that life will smile at you."

Her words were a source of energy and inspiration. I really wanted to overcome those resistances inside myself:

"And how can I practically cope with my fears Doc?"

"A very powerful tool, and also very beautiful, is being in touch with your inner child. Reflect, a child is not afraid. They fall and get up again. We lose all of this because the world in general puts fears, mostly non-existent, on us and so if we "fall" we feel like failures and at that point we don't even risk things anymore. In this way, we stop our growth. Fear immobilizes us. The little girl inside of you exists and when you are hurt by these fears you suffer. This work consists of going towards her to comfort her. Let's do it right away. Close your eyes Paola, do three deep breaths, relax and try to enter with the eyes of the mind inside your heart. Where is that little girl inside of you? Can you see her? How is she?"

"She's scared, she's a little sad and she feels lonely. She is all curled up in herself and she isn't smiling."

"Look at her with love, smile and tell her: "It's all right, you're safe, you and I are one. From now on I will take care of you, you will not be alone anymore, come to play with me! Always remember that you deserve to be loved!" Now hug her, make her feel protected. Stay with her for a while, see what happens and, when you're ready, calmly open your eyes."

"What a nice job doctor!" I exclaimed with joy. "I had never thought that there was this little child inside of me. It was important to console her and be near her, I feel much better!"

"Go to see her more often Paola. Children need love, affection, smiles and protection."

This work with myself had left me with a sense of tranquility and serenity. It was as if I had looked into my fears from a different point of view. I realized that fear often does not truly exist, it's actually worry regardless of an existing problem, which we feed and which blocks our evolution. With this new awareness I faced the World Championship in Portimao. Unlike the year before, when everything had happened casually, I was more centered and I knew what I wanted. I had more confidence, and I combined physical work with mental work as usual.

The competition itself was not perfect, I felt the tension and external expectations. After the compulsory dances, I occupied the second position but the games were still open and I knew that with a good free dance I could recover, as I did the year before.

After the pre-competition warm-up, the national athletic trainer came up to me and said: "Your musculature is not very suitable for a figure skater." I took that badly and thought it was a completely inappropriate statement for him to have made before I entered the rink to face the World Final. But I decided to take it as a further challenge and to show him that he was wrong. Anger is a very strong emotion. If channeled in the right direction it can turn into a positive and powerful energy that could be useful in a difficult moment. I did exactly that. The provocation of that person allowed me to pull out even more grit.

It was time to compete and face the challenge. My mother, at the edge of the rink with me, said: "Paola you are here to give the best of yourself, you're ready! Bring all of your own power. Go and dance... There is only you and the music, don't think of anything, just have fun."

To enjoy was the key idea that had given me the win in my first World Championship. Before entering I patted my leg repeating: "Go Paola, have fun!"

Since then I have always done this before starting a competition. It is a gesture that makes me enter in the right state of mind: Competition On. It's called an "anchor" in "NLP," (Neuro-linguistic Programming) or an association process of a physical sensation to an internal response. I didn't know that at the time however. I did it instinctively, almost like a superstitious gesture and with this spirit I entered the rink.

My program was a crescendo. I started a little quietly but with every note, trust and relaxation increased. I was trying to turn off my brain and just enjoy the moment. The music and me, just us. And even this time, when I finished, the public supported me with applause. I was filled with an indescribable energy.

Coming off the rink my mom smiled and when I arrived she hugged me really tight. At the same time the score came out and Place 1 was on the screen!

Once again I was the World Champion, exhausted but so satisfied by the announcement of victory. On the podium, the Italian anthem played for me. From the highest step, I saw again the year of training, travel, train hours, courses and work. But everything at that moment had a

reason. I had been rewarded for all the sacrifices I had endured.

Sacrificing does not mean renouncing, but making
sacred something.
Make what you love sacred and you will manifest
the most divine part of you.

Chapter 5

2011 New Awareness

Winning Mental Attitude and Anchors

After my second World Championship, and the Masters in Sports Psychology in Milan, I understood the value of the mental component in achieving goals and I wanted to know more and more. I kept on studying but I had little time available. Training between Rome and Genoa was seriously intense.

Constantly traveling, by train or by plane, I was struggling to reconcile work and having a social life with skating.

I was tired. My physiological functions had stopped, I hadn't had my period for months, I was full of pimples, I put on weight and I couldn't sleep well. I had literally arrived to nearly a point of no return.

I had to put that crazy lifestyle on hold for at least a week. So I took the courage to tell everyone: "Sorry but I'm sick, I need to stop for a moment because otherwise I will not be able to get to the Italian Championships." It was difficult to admit that I had had enough, I don't like to miss training, but it was the only thing to do in order to refuel, recharge and deal with both competitions: single and couple at the best of my abilities.

I often forget myself. I'm so inside the vortex of life and consumed by what I have to do, that my body has to send me clear signs to stop. The doctor always tells me: "Paola you have to put yourself on a pedestal and understand that you are there before everything else. You must treat yourself well. You're not a robot. Take time to rest and recover. Remember that to enlighten others you must first of all illuminate yourself, you must be at the center of the sun, not on the radius." It's true. Too many times I forget to first find that energy in myself to be able to give it to others.

Being alive only for others leads to forgetting about yourself...

If you are the Sun, your rays illuminate everyone,
But if you are in the rays, you don't enlighten anyone,
not even yourself.
The center gives you the vital energy.
It keeps you stable and at the rudder of your life.

With this awareness I decided to take a week off in May and go to Fuerteventura with my brother and my dear friend Emanuela.

I'm usually active on the beach. I like to play, run and stay in the water, but during that week I didn't do any of that. I didn't have the strength. I was lying down, eating, sleeping, reading, enjoying the sun and some gentle walks; nothing more. It was the only way to recharge my batteries. Listening to your body is the first step to loving yourself. In fact, after that trip, my body took back all the physiological functions it had lost. Even the training went better and I finally had more energy to give.

For my free dance in solos I had decided to prepare the choreography to the music of Rio, the animation film released the same year, 2011. The World Championships would have been held in Brazil and it seemed a great co-incidence. The work in Rome was quite intense and I dedicated more time to the couple than to the solo.

That's why I trained a lot mentally, spending the hours on the train visualizing my success.

Despite the week of vacation in May, I arrived at the end of July without energy. I was probably exhausted after the two years of travel, work and training.

I was in Rome and it was extremely hot. We practiced outdoors, sometimes under the scorching July sun. Traveling between Genoa and Rome every week left me with no time to go to the doctor. When I arrived in Roccaraso for the Italian Championships, I collapsed on the bed and I slept for two hours straight even though it was four o'clock in the afternoon.

The couple and single competitions overlapped so I had several performances all in one day. Both single and couple compulsory dances went well but the following day I had a breakdown. The original dance for couples wasn't exceptional, we couldn't give our best and we lost a position. My free dance of singles was fine but I was not fully satisfied.

The choreography was very intense, fast and still new to me because I had only prepared it a few weeks before. Despite everything, I won and qualified for the World Championships in Brazil.

The day after, before the free dance in pairs, during the official trial, when lifting me up, Marco inadvertently hit me with his elbow in a point between my nose and my eye. It was a strong bump, my eye began to darken and my head was spinning. Despite the accident, we placed in fourth position.

This meant no World Championships but we could have access to the European Championships in Reggio Calabria, in September. All that remained was to train for that goal.

After the Italian Championships, it was clear to me that I couldn't go on living like this. I spent the first two weeks of August on a real vacation; sea, mountains, friends and sleep. I did what in two years of training between Genoa and Rome I had never done. Simple things but so necessary.

My parents always taught me to do everything seriously and with commitment but they also wanted me to live my life freely and I'm immensely grateful for this. I went to high school, scouts and I took vacations with friends. For me, it has always been important to find the time to have a chat with friends, to visit places, compare myself with others. I reload and then I take the baggage of my life on the skating rink and I transform it in emotions. I don't agree with the idea of living just for your sport and I understood that especially during the two years of training in Rome. However important they were for my growth, I realized that I came out of those years completely exhausted.

It was during that August that I met Marco for the first time, my boyfriend with whom I shared several important years. With him everything was simple and natural from the beginning. Being with him gave me loads of positive energy. During that time, I was ready to experience a deep relationship and I wanted one. I thought about it for some time and in the previous years I had focused a lot on myself because in my personal life I only had disappointments.

When something generally disappoints us, we often close the door and turn our gaze to what could reward us more. Distracting ourselves is a sort of unconscious protection. I had focused on skating and personal growth.

Regarding this, I read a book about a neuro-linguistics program in which it said:

What you focus on becomes your reality.

That is, what you place your attention and energy on is destined to manifest in your life. It can seem trivial, but we often focus on our default patterns. Even Max Gentile had reiterated the same concept, summarized in this scheme that I always remember because it is applicable to any field of life:

RESULTS <-> ACTIONS <-> MOOD

The results, positive or negative, depend on our actions, in turn are guided by our state of mind.

If we are calm and relaxed it will be easier to act and get positive results. On the contrary, if we are agitated, confused and pessimistic, our actions, and therefore the results, will tend to be mediocre.

INSTRUMENTS: MENTAL FOCUS, INTERNAL LANGUAGE, PHYSIOLOGY

Our mood is in turn influenced by 3 fundamental aspects:

1. Mental Focus

2. Internal Language

3. Physiology

Mental Focus

Mental focus is the ability of the mind to orient itself to one thing in particular. It allows you to speed up tasks, respond promptly to solicitations and increase concentration. What you are mentally focusing on, automatically or consciously, grows and manifests.

If you don't use your will, your mental focus will tend to orientate itself according to previous patterns and routines. For example, if a person is brought up to focus on problems, they are likely to only see problems and not the solutions. I had started to focus my mind on an emotional relationship. I had written down the characteristics of my "ideal Man:" Fun, Cute, Affectionate, Intelligent, Full of Surprises, Dynamic, a Traveler, Smiley and Naturally Ready to Share Himself and Live in a Harmonious Relationship with Me...

In this way, I had focused part of my energies on those specific things. I often read and re-read the list and imagined my future boyfriend as if he existed, and... he had arrived.

This mental process occurs in every aspect of life. Have you ever thought of a specific person and then received a call from them soon after? Or when you want to buy a new model of a car and then you start seeing that specific model on the road all the time? This happens because you are focused on a determined thought and you start to attract what you place attention on. So don't let your thoughts go in a random direction. Decide to focus your mind on constructive, positive, dedicated thoughts. In this way, your mood will be better and it will lead you to act in ways which achieve positive results.

Taking the example of sports: if before a competition you focus your thoughts on a fall that previously happened, your mood will not be the best. On the contrary, if you turn your thoughts to a moment of victory, you will immediately feel better and the actions you will take will bring you more easily to achieving what you want.

Sending energy towards your final result is a way for you to attract the result itself.

Your mental focus must be like the compass that always follows true north despite the circumstances.

The only athlete you are destined to become is the athlete that YOU decide to be!

Internal Language

Another aspect that influences the result is the internal language, or how we speak with ourselves.

Consciously or unconsciously, we talk and talk to ourselves. These things that we "say" can drastically affect our reality.

How do you talk to yourself during training, before or during a competition? Try asking yourself and pay attention. Your internal language, as well as your mental focus, are fundamental to achieving the results that you want to achieve.

Before knowing it, I let my mind go in a certain direction without controlling it. "What if I can't do it? The rink is slippery, everyone is falling down! That athlete is better than me!" While I inwardly talked to myself like that, my anxiety was rising, I was becoming more agitated and consequently my actions and results reflected my words.

When I understood it, I decided to focus on what I was saying and whenever my words started to take me into a negative mood, I began change my self-talk and then would repeat a new personal mantra: "I can!"

In repeating this over and over again, my energy rose back up and I was more positive and concentrated to better face the competition. Not only during the warm up and before the competition, but also in training. This mantra has changed my mood many times. If in your mind you keep repeating that you can't do it, that you are incapable and it is not for you, you will do nothing but reinforce your belief. Record this belief in the brain and it will only come true. What you constantly repeat to yourself is inevitably what you will believe.

So every time your brain goes automatically towards a self-destructive thought, try to reverse it and tell yourself: "It's all right, I can do it!"

Exercise

Repeat for a minute: "I can! I have all the skills to reach my goals!" and for another minute: "I'm a failure, I only mess up."

How do you feel after the first minute? I imagine: energetic, strong and empowered, ready to conquer the world.

Instead after the next one probably sad and demoralized. Am I wrong?

The way we talk influences our mood.

Physiology

Finally, your thoughts affect your physiology and your physiology influences your thoughts. If your body assumes an open posture: head up, deep and calm breathing, your thoughts will automatically become more positive and triumphant!

Even if your morale is low, try to jump up and down, clap your hands upwards and boldly smile! I'm sure you'll feel better right away! Try to laugh and think of something sad at the same time. You will realize that it is particularly difficult. This is to make you understand how much you can actually control your state of mind and your emotions. If before a competition you are worried or anxious, or you can't calm down, try to tell to yourself several times: "It's all right, I can do it!" And meanwhile breathe deeply, open your shoulders and raise your head up! Before a competition, don't look to the ground, don't close yourself up. On the contrary, try two minutes of positive internal language and your body, without a doubt, will reflect your thoughts: open your shoulders, breathe deeply and relaxed, be determined and channel your energy in the right way.

In summary: your results, positive or negative, depend on your actions, which also depend on your positive or negative state of mind. In turn, they are influenced by internal language, physiology and by mental focus. Verify in your daily life what I've explained here. Every time you get a result check the previous action and review the mental mechanism underlined:

Result:

––

Action:

––

Mood:

––

How was I talking to myself? Where was my focus/attention? What was my posture like?

If your mental attitude is triumphant it will be easier to get positive results.

Having experienced the effect of this new awareness myself, I obtained great results. We won the European title in couples and everything went wonderfully from the beginning to the end of the competition.

2011 World Championships

That year Genoa was particularly hit by a sudden change in atmospheric conditions. A very intense flood damaged our skating rink. The water had reached almost 7 feet destroying everything that was in the changing rooms, the gym and in the office. Mud, branches and leaves had slipped everywhere. The surface of the rink was in ruins. The center remained closed for a week to put everything back in order. The physical preparation for the World Championships was therefore, in part, compromised but I continued with the mental one. I took the opportunity to go to the doctor with whom I'd established the battle plan.

"Doctor, I'm a little worried because I'm not training a lot. I had to skip some sessions because of the flood. But I'm working off of skates and I'm taking some Samba classes as well. Mentally I'm doing visualizations, I'm working on my beliefs, I write in my diary every day and this gives me the opportunity to see what is going through my mind and let the emotions out. In general I feel good, even the relationship with Marco makes me very happy but at the same time I'm afraid of not being focused enough on the competition."

"Because it's a new thing that clearly destabilizes you but it also gives you positive energy, doesn't it?"

"Yes, sure! I'm used to my independence and sometimes I'm afraid of losing it."

"You see Paola, you just have to get organized! Dedicate time to your preparation, but make sure you enjoy yourself and also the moments you spend with him. Get the positive energy that you will then take onto the rink during training. Do not be afraid of the beautiful things that are happening, but above all, do not be afraid of the changes that have to take place inside of you. The fear of not being focused on the competition is real but I think it comes from your fear of getting involved in a new situation... Am I wrong?"

She hit the target. I was worried about changing my habits. I had won the last two World Championships focusing only on myself and now that there was another person, I was afraid of being destabilized.

"That's so true! We are bogged down in our habits and we struggle without them!"

"It's right! But do not be drastic. Habits make us feel good, give us security and are like rituals that you can use in your favor. In this regard, I want to talk to you about anchors."

"Yes, I know what you're talking about, but I've never worked on this intentionally. Tell me in more detail doctor!"

"It's a NLP technique. Anchoring means fixing on an internal state for the purpose of reproducing it in an automatic way when the anchor is activated. We are involuntarily full of anchors: names, objects, places, even perfumes are anchors. Has it ever happened to you to smell a certain scent that reminds you of something or someone? Or find yourself in a place that automatically gives you a sense of peace?"

"Yes, absolutely! Even objects often remind me of something familiar and seeing them triggers a certain mood."

"Exactly! Today I want to create an anchor with you that will bring you back to the state of mind of the World's victory last year, or the year before, so you can use it at the next championship. You can use any gesture, any movement, but I'm suggesting this because it's particularly practical. Put your index fingertip and the tip of your thumb on your right hand together and squeeze them as if you are holding something between them. Now close your eyes and imagine the moment of the awards ceremony of last year's World Championship. Enter inside of it, relive the situation, how did you feel? What did you feel? What did you see? How did you breathe? What was your mood?

Fix the image inside of you, feel it and squeeze the two fingers together. Associate that gesture with what you're imagining and feeling. Now, go to the 2009 awards and do the same thing with your fingertips. Remain in this state for a while and continue tightening the two fingers. When you're ready, open your eyes and let go of your fingers!"

I opened my eyes and it was as if time had stopped.

She went on: "Now tighten your two fingers again and tell me if you can relive those same emotions even with your eyes opened."

"Yes, I can!"

"Very well, this is one more tool you have at your disposal. You must continue to train, do the same exercise we did together every day. Start by using this anchor even during training, so you can also use it in the competition. Make it become a positive habit that will take you into a victorious state of mind."

"I will certainly do it."

"I'm sure you already have your rituals, even though perhaps you are not aware of them, but this is something more. You can voluntarily go to that particular mood now."

"It's true, I call them "good luck charms," but they are effectively rituals because they allow me to concentrate on the moment and enter the competition mode. For example, I always do my laces the same way, I do my exercises to warm up, and when I enter the rink, I give two taps of my right leg and I repeat: "Go Paola, have fun!" I think these are already anchors, right?"

"Exactly! You see, these are positive habits that bring you into the right mood to face the competition! Call them good luck charms if you prefer, but we are talking about anchors! ...And I want to give you a little tip: since you're doing a lot of training off of skates, when you try your choreography, close your eyes. By doing this you will feel much more aware of yourself in your body and the sensations that the anchor gives you. And if there is a part that worried you, try to do it in slow motion. Your body will learn faster."

"That's so interesting! I'll try for sure! Thank you!"

"Paola remember that you are worthy, you have all the tools to be the World Champion again!"

I was ready and particularly happy because for the first time I was flying overseas. After Germany and Portugal, going to Brazil made me feel like I was in the dimension of a true World Championship. I was expecting the heat and the festive atmosphere. I had my own ideas in mind but this expectation collapsed immediately when I saw the skating rink. A 1960's building, without changing rooms. It was quite cold and the sky was always grey. There were only three hours time difference compared to Italy, but I felt them all. I used to wake up at five in the morning and at eight o'clock at night I was collapsing in bed. But I was often training past eleven o'clock. I was tired, under stress and I had a strong pain in my legs.

My mother and brother arrived, and even they were shattered after an endless journey. My mom had swelling and fluid retention in her legs and Matteo, as soon as he arrived, had an illness that lasted for twelve hours. They published the order to enter the rink and it wasn't the best one for me. In the second dance I would enter first and the group of the strongest athletes were to come out after me. Basically, at that moment, I thought I had misplaced my expectations on Brazil.

I sensed a strange energy. I didn't feel like participating in a World Championship and I didn't feel ready to enter the competition. The training proceeded well but not at my maximum. I was tired, and the negative emotions were amplified by my exhaustion. Everything seemed more difficult and I couldn't see the bright side. In fact, I wasn't able to give much of myself at all in the first compulsory dance.

I came out aware of this and the score wasn't high. My mother came to me and said: "Paola this is just the beginning, from now on don't be stupid, go in and do what you know how to do!"

She was right, I just had to do what I knew without worrying about all the negative circumstances.

That year the World Championship was like that, I didn't have control on the rink, nor on the venue and the entrance line up. I had to accept the situation. The only thing I could do was focus again.

With open shoulders and a high head, I began to repeat: "I can do it and I deserve it!"

I had found the goal again. I went out first in the second dance, a tango, and I managed to transform the anger I felt inside into a very powerful energy. I was back! I was totally me again! The score was good but the mistake in the first dance did not allow me to position myself at the top of the ranking. As in previous years, I had to rise up with the free dance. Giving the maximum, I could still take back my place, the distance was definitely recoverable.

The following morning, after the official trial, I turned to my mother and said: "You brought me the dress, right?" I had left it with her the day before because the embroidering needed to be finished. She grabbed the bag, looked everywhere but couldn't find it.

"But where did I put it? I'm sure I took it before I left!" Suddenly, wide-eyed, she looked at me and said: "Oh my God, Paola! I left it in the taxi!" She sat down without strength, incredulous and pale, with a lost gaze. I tried to reassure her: "Don't worry mom, I can put on the trial dress and nothing will happen!"

My brother tried to take matters into his own hands: "Let's call the central taxi station, maybe they've found it!" After several attempts in vain to call, my mother's phone finally rang: the dress was fortunately found and they would bring it back to the skating rink. This absurd situation had the power to wake me up from the torpor hovering in my mind from the day before, I felt that things were getting back on track.

When I was at the hotel, my brother sent me a message: "Paola, you are the Queen, everyone cheers for you! Go and enchant the whole world as only you can do!"

I received messages of encouragement and, when I arrived on the rink there was a huge surprise, Marco was waiting for me with a sunflower in his hand. Now everyone was really there, both in Brazil and from home.

I knew I had to come down to win my personal battle once again. As a good warrior I prepared myself with all my rituals, I was entering my competition mode and, unlike the day before, the energies played in my favor.

I held the thumb and forefinger of my right hand close, squeezed strong and I was back at the awards ceremony of the previous years. I wanted to live that emotion again and give it to people who were watching and supporting me. I entered the rink giving myself the two taps on the leg and with my mother's voice repeated: "Go like a lion Paola!"

It was time to live the magic and let myself go to the samba rhythm.

Brazilians supported me with applause at the rhythm of the music and I enjoyed myself a lot. I left the rink happy, knowing that I had done my best. In truth, our best is the only thing we can do. The score was high and Place 1 appeared once more on the screen!

I had done it! I had started on the wrong foot, but during the competition I knew how to change the course of it and aim to achieve my goal. I had learned not to let myself go in the circumstances, to react to the situation; to channel the anger and turn it into energy that would work in my favor. The Italian anthem was played once again for me and for all of the people who had supported me with all their love and affection.

You'll be amazed at what you attract after you start believing in what you deserve.

Chapter 6

2012

Clarify and Reach Objectives

"**P**aola, what do you think you're going to do now that you've won three World Championships?" My mom asked me, once we were home from Brazil.

"Well! I think I may win a fourth." I replied.

"Wow, you're not giving up, eh? That's fine, but how do you want to reach your goal?"

This question made me reflect. I understood that winning the fourth World Championship was only the final destination, but how would I get there? Every year, to win, I had to create something innovative, I had to be superior to the others so that any possible doubt on the judges' side was debunked. To get there I had to be strong technically, choreographically and mentally.

That year, for the free dance, I decided to choose the music from the opera Carmen by Bizet. I also asked a really good choreographer in Trieste, Sandro Guerra, to give me some suggestions and support in the creation of the piece.

My long-term goal was to win the fourth World Championship. I had to identify which steps I should take to confirm the title again and in which order.

My mental coach, Max, helped me in this process.

I remember that initially my motivation wasn't solid. I wanted to continue skating but, after having won three Championships, keeping the title always required more effort. The Brazilian World Championship had cost me so much in terms of fatigue, I was tired. With my boyfriend Marco I was feeling great and I wanted to spend more time with him.

Basically, I went through a critical phase in which I needed an external support to find my way.

So I asked him:"To set a goal is easy but sometimes it's difficult for me to keep my motivation high. I had to stop couples because I spent more time on the train than on the skating rink. After three World Championships and all the difficulties I have had, like the lack of an adequate rink in Genoa, the fact that I work so hard to support my skating... I'm determined but believe me, sometimes it's tough."

"I believe you Paola, you are a human being too!" he answered, laughing. "Apart from everything, I understand you fully and my advice is to set clear objectives with a deadline, but do not stop, understand inside of you if your thoughts and beliefs are in line with the goals themselves. You have to believe it with every cell of your body otherwise it will get worse, as it has already happened in the past. But let's start from the beginning. First, when you start an activity, whether in sports or any other, it is necessary to set goals that respect the S.M.A.R.T sequence:

- Specific, that is clear and defined, that doesn't leave space for ambiguity.

- Measurable, so you can verify it at any time.

- Achievable, since a non-achievable objective demotivates you to act the same way as you would do for one too easily reached. This is the point that will keep your motivation high.

- Relevant, from an organizational point of view, so it is in line with your mission.

- Timed, i.e. with a deadline, make sure your brain is programmed to achieve the goal itself.

"Can you help me to do this? I have always written my goals in the training diary to get them constantly in view. It's an exercise I've already done, even in the past few years, but if you guide me I'm sure that I will make a huge leap!"

"Of course, it's a pleasure. My advice is to set short, medium and long-term goals.

Initially decide the long term ones, 3 to 5 months away, and then ask to yourself this question: "How do I achieve those goals?" This makes it easier to identify short-term goals, 2 weeks to 1 month away, and medium-term goals, 2 to 3 months away. Our brain needs an expiration date. If it knows that within that date it must get that result, it will be organized to get it."

I opened my 2012 training diary and I started to write my long-term goals:

1. Win the Italian Championship of Solo Dance in Roccaraso.

2. Win the Solo Dance World Championship in Auckland.

3. Receive a perfect score of 10 (because until then I've never reached the maximum score).

"Well Paola, your goals are very clear. Now answer this question: how do you get there? What are the small steps you need to take to get there? If your road is clear it will be easier to reach the goal. Let's start working on the first one because the Italian Championship comes before the World one."

I immediately started writing:

> *Short term -> go to Sandro, my choreographer, review the free dance and finish it both technically and artistically.*

> *For the compulsory dances: improve the first part of the quickstep and make it smoother. In the waltz, take over an open posture and stretch my legs more.*
> *Technically improve the edges in both dances.*

> *Medium term -> work more on the free dance from an emotional point of view. Take flamenco lessons. Enter into the character doing research, watching videos and possibly go to see Carmen by Bizet live.*
> *Technically, make it even more fluid and solid.*

> *Work mentally on the fact that I can be at the top of the ranking already after the compulsory dances.*
> *Improve presentation and communicate confidence.*

"Very good, these are the steps you need to do to get to the Italian Championship. Are you ready to do all of this?"

To have written down what I had to do gave me a sense of tranquility and confidence.

Sometimes what remains to be done seems more difficult than it actually is.

"Yes, of course, but I don't want to self-sabotage any-more. I'm tired of always experience something difficult before a competition, whether it's a pain somewhere or a sudden event that complicates the journey."

"You hit the point!" He said smiling. "To write down your goals is just the first part of the work. Now you have to understand if there is some belief inside of you that blocks you from achieving the goals themselves. Answer this question: why do you think you sabotage yourself?"

I didn't know what to say, I had no idea.

"I asked you Max!"

"No Paola, the answer is yours. I can direct you, but you are the one who must find the key to access your re-sources."

I took a deep breath and started talking without think-ing too much.

"You see Max, I think sometimes there's something inside of me that blocks me. I believe that to reach some-thing I always have to work hard otherwise it would be too insignificant. It's like I have to climb a mountain every time and, believe me, I'm exhausted."

"Ok stop!" Max told me. "You said something very important: I believe that to achieve something myself I always have to work hard. Right?"

I nodded.

"This is the answer, the limiting belief that guides you to your self-sabotage."

I opened my eyes wide, remembering the work on my beliefs that I had already done in the past and realized that this was yet another weakening belief.

"Help me to change it Max, please, I can't anymore. I want to do the competitions in serenity. I'm exhausted from this constant battle with myself."

"Take your training diary, divide the pages in two

and write your limiting belief on the left hand side. Read it, and turn it into an empowering belief like: *I can reach my goals with simplicity and serenity.* Or find a sentence that motivates you and replace your negative belief with it."

So I did and wrote in large letters on the right of the sheet: *"I deserve to reach my goals easily and everything will be fine!"*

"It's amazing how much our belief system guides our lives and most of the time we don't even acknowledge what we believe in."

"Yeah, that's right, that's why I'm telling you to do this exercise: go home and write on the left part of the sheet all the beliefs that come to your mind, in any field of your life, not just about sports. What you believe about family, your romantic relationship, work, age, friends... Write, and if you find a belief that takes away from your energy, transform it into positive statement as we have done today. Then read them every day until you create a kind of "confusion" in your mind. To put doubt in a belief is the first step to weaken it and leave room for a new positive one. Remember that the brain works through habits and repetition: if you constantly repeat the new belief for at least twenty days, you'll see that something will change.

Let's recap! Remember that it is not enough to put the goal down and think that everything will come by itself, it doesn't work like that. Setting up the goal is only the first step. Once you have set your goal, have decided the deadline, and have planned how to get it, there is a subtle but fundamental step: are you sure your unconscious really agrees with what you want rationally?

Let's take an example: your rational part seeks the goal of winning the National Championships. You're absolutely resolute and you commit yourself with all your strength to achieve it, but your unconscious part believes that winning is dangerous for you, that basically you don't deserve to win, or the victory would mean being different from others, or that you don't have enough trust in your skills. In this case, rational and non-rational don't coincide, and given that the unconscious is like a stubborn child who always wants to be right, you will never win the National Championship if you don't convince that child that you can do it and that you deserve all the victories in the world. Maybe you train like a crazy person, you're physically ready, you have all the potential to arrive there but, coincidentally, a few days before the competition you twist your foot and can't give it your best. Your unconscious has sabotaged you. This defeat leads to discouragement. At best, with patience, you can start all over again. But in the worst case, you abandon everything, accusing the bad luck, the coach, the judges, the system, etc. Well, I have some news to give you: bad luck doesn't exist! If you are concentrated on you and you are aware of how things are going, you'll never blame the circumstances. You must be aware of your choices at all times and always be responsible for your actions."

*A champion is one who acts with confidence
despite the circumstances.*

I was always going back to Max's words. Circumstances cannot interfere with your performance if you are really centered; or at least they shouldn't be a reason to justify yourself, but rather a stimulus and a challenge. Finally, I understood the reason of certain injuries and situations which always happen with a precise meaning. My unconscious had tried to sabotage me many times. Before 2009

I didn't know anything about this. I was training physically but the only mental training I was doing were little random visualizations. In the competition, I wasn't great. I didn't transmit confidence, I didn't feel good enough to win, I panicked, I lost energy looking at others and listening to everyone's thoughts. I was not concentrated on me. I was ready to be defeated.

Max continued: "An indispensable characteristic Paola, is the resoluteness. Being resolute means reaching your goal, at any cost. Yes, it is all too easy to surrender to the first difficulty and find excuses like: "In the end it's not for me, I thought it would have been different, I'm not made for these things..." As you well know, it's not always easy, sometimes yes, but sometimes you have to fight to reach a positive result. It takes energy and it's hard, but it's worth it, because once the goal is achieved you will be a different person, more aware and more mature. Life put trials in front of us, crises and obstacles to overcome, otherwise we would always be at the same point and our evolution would stop when we're still children. Do you think perhaps that children do not struggle when they learn to walk, talk and eat alone? Yet, they try, they fall, they make mistakes, they don't give up and they try again. Everyone can do it. If we can do it as children, now who are we? Are we any different? Must adults have everything immediately? Reflect on this, it is crucial. If you don't immediately find the solution, make attempts, try another way, and look for new ideas to get there."

"It's true, this is a really fundamental point Max, and I hardly ever give up. Fortunately, I'm very determined and until I reach the goal, I give all of myself. After all I'm an Aries!" I replied smiling.

"I know, otherwise you would have never arrived here, but many people are struggling and I'm sure it happened to you as well to help you live through your moments of discouragement."

"Absolutely, and now I'm in one of these phases. I know I have to find the resources inside of me to raise myself up, to implement new strategies, to continue to evolve in my sports career and in my life.

When I was young, before going onto the rink, my mom always told me: "Get the grit you have inside of you Paola! Let me see the lion!" And I used to imitate the roar and make a combative position. This is a playful attitude that was useful when I needed to get out the grit in difficult moments. It lead me to be the lion, not the gazelle."

"What you're telling me is very significant, your mom planted the belief in you: take the difficulty as a challenge, fight and don't give up! Beautiful!" He replied.

"Yes, it's true, I have never thought about it. In fact, I struggle with the difficulties, however, as I told you before, sometimes I'm tired of always being at war!"

"You will see that working on your new belief, everything will be better and, as you already know, the key that will help you to reach your goals faster will be the visualizations."

I knew how to visualize. I had done it for years and I had achieved incredible results, but I had never done a routine so specific about goals, beliefs and visualizations. Visualizing my new belief, associated with the outcome of the competition, would have been a new experience and it would have made me reach the result much more easily.

"Max, I've been practicing visualizing for years now, but can you give me some extra suggestions and explain better how it works?"

INSTRUMENTS: ADVANCED VISUALIZATION
PART II

"The visualization must be as real as possible, as if you had taken a dip into the future and lived intensely what you want to achieve, entering completely inside it and living everything in advance. Listen, touch, feel, enjoy and above all experience the emotions entirely. Imagine that it will go exactly as you want. It is necessary that you feel it and live it as if everything is real. What do you feel? Who is with you? How do you address yourself? What is your facial expression?

This creates a new neural pathway. Imagine having a field with tall grass in front of you. If you walk on this back and forth, every day, always in the same way, soon you will form a beaten path and, when the time comes to decide which way to go, it will be easier to take the one you already know, the one you have walked many times. The same thing happens in life. If you create your path in advance in your brain, through the visualization, and mentally go through the same story for one month, when it happens in real life, it will be easier to follow what you already know. It will be like living the experience again. It is important to prepare for the event and to not leave anything to chance. It is like arriving in a new city not knowing where to go to get to the hotel. If you have informed yourself before the departure that once you're at the airport you have to take the bus, get off at the seventh stop, walk for about 600 feet and turn right, it will be difficult for you to lose and waste time. If instead you know nothing, you'll have to start asking. You can go wrong and get to the hotel in twice the time. You'll get there eventually, but you won't know how and it could be much riskier.

The same happens for the events in your life. Get ready, live them in advance and direct your mind and intentions towards what you want to obtain. If you want everything to go smoothly before your competition, you won't have to do anything else but visualize your calm and peaceful mood and see that with this mental and physical peace you can face anything.

I'm sure everything will go better for the next competition and you will no longer feel this sense of duty to climb the mountains to achieve the positive result."

"Thank you for this explanation and thank you for this meeting. I really feel a lot more motivated, I want to work on my limitations and make a huge leap this year."

An important belief came to the surface that would later make the difference in competitions. I went home and started writing down what I thought about the different areas of my life like Max had suggested. A few sentences came out and I didn't know where they came from.

Beliefs are at the helm of our life and if we don't solve them they will take us in the same direction and probably will lead us to make the same mistakes for a long time. Beliefs govern our mind; they are our truths. We accept them unconditionally, basing all of our judgments on that system, even when it comes to choices that go against our nature.

But sooner or later the man who wins is the one
who believes he can.
Napoleon Hill

Our belief system is formed during childhood.

It comes from parents, relatives, friends, teachers and experiences that we have experienced and that have left a mark on us. It touches every area of our life. For this reason, even today, every three months or so, I take my notebook and I write down what I think about myself, work, love, friends, success, money...

Whenever I have a doubt about any context, I write, and every time I am amazed. To correct a limiting belief with an empowering one gives me surprising results.

World Championships 2012

I had worked a lot, both mentally and physically, and I had hit all my goals. At the Italian Championship I was already in first place before the compulsory dances and in the free dance I received perfect 10s for the artistic content.

Immersed in the flow of the dance, I relived the inner state that I had experimented with in Freiburg, when everything went perfectly up until the conclusion, without me even realizing how.

Sometimes this happened even while I was training. This magical state used to persist even during the night.

In the summer I went to Verona to see the opera Carmen live. It greatly inspired me and helped me to more deeply create and become the character.

That year the World Championships would be held at the beginning of October in Auckland, New Zealand. I only set medium-term goals for myself because there were only two months left.

Before leaving, the doctor gave me some great advice that I used several times: "Dear Paola if, in the middle of the competition, self-sabotaging thoughts come to your mind, start singing the music you are dancing to. In this way you will distract the rational mind and free yourself from all the worries."

"That's great! I love this tip! I'll try for sure."

"Have a great competition! And try to rest during the flight! It's really long and you'll need to be ready right away since you're going to compete the next day!"

"I will for sure! Thanks so much Doc! I'll send you a message to keep you updated!"

I was really happy to go across the world and see a place so far away from Italy. The journey was long but I love reading, writing and watching movies. A long journey is also a time when you are forced to stop and do things that in everyday life often you neglect due to a lack of time. Because it was so far from Italy, it seemed that nobody could come to see me but, my mom did something crazy and, in the end, booked a flight to come.

I was so happy to have her at the side of the rink and to be able to share this experience with her one more time. Marco also, came to see me on the final day. Everyone was following me from home, even at night.

The most important people in my life were with me, even if some of them were physically distant. The World Championship in Auckland was special.

I remember that from the second day I received unequivocal signs. I climbed on top of the Sky Tower, the highest in the southern hemisphere!

Walking through the shops inside the tower, I saw a large globe that was exactly like a pendant that we had gifted to my grandmother years before. Both during the competition and on different occasions in my life, I felt her strong presence. I'm sure she is always with me and that sometimes she manifests herself with small signs. Sometimes through flowers, sometimes with names or words, others in dreams, and this gives me the sense that I am never alone, especially in the most challenging moments. That globe told me that she was there and that, even this time, she was supporting me.

The trials before the competition went well. I was

ready, even if a little worried, because a very good, strong American World Junior Champion was participating and was joined by several coaches. I was trying to stay focused on me, I repeated *I will succeed* and I gathered all of my concentration before the competition. When I could, I was going on walks alone, I put earphones in and mentally competed to the music. I was entering my world and turning off all the external voices that removed my energy.

We must protect ourselves as much as possible from external influences when dealing with a challenge.

As much as I was happy to be there, I always had the feeling like I wanted to escape. This had also happened on previous occasions. I didn't feel completely aligned and present, and my unconscious mind was pushing me to leave. I didn't know how to handle it, until the solution arrived: the night before the competition I had a really significant dream. A friend from the national team proposed to return to Italy because he was tired of being there and I replied: "Why not? Let's go back to Italy!"

My dad and my brother had welcomed me with joy but, after a while, I realized that this wasn't my place at the time.

My brother told me: "What are you doing here? Why are you back? And now what are you going to tell to the national team staff?"

I was getting worse, I was anguished, I saw Auckland and everything in New Zealand as an incredible place yet there I was in Italy, far away. I was realizing that I had thrown everything to the wind. I wanted to teleport myself and return back in the blink of an eye. I woke up suddenly. I realized, thank goodness, I was in Auckland for real. When awake, my anguish vanished fully. That dream had freed me completely from the fear of entering the rink that very often annoyed me before competitions, and the unconscious desire to run away. I no longer felt the same unpleasant feeling. I was now concentrated without the fear of entering the rink and with the sense of fully wanting to be there.

For the first time, I could face the compulsory dances with confidence, not by chance, I was already in first position after the first part. The feeling was beautiful and absolutely new. This time I didn't have to recover, I just had to do well and keep my position. The next day there was the free dance, the *Carmen* that had scored me a unanimous 10 for artistic content in the Italian Championship.

Meanwhile, Marco also joined me. I knew that so many people were connecting back home via streaming on the internet at 4:00 AM their time to watch me and cheer me on. Before the competition, I went with Marco to the cafe to buy water for me and a sandwich for him. I remember sitting at table number 4 and, at that moment, I recognized the sign: I would win the fourth World Championship! Whoever has experienced the sensation of "Talking signals" knows what it feels like. It is a sudden and inexplicable intuition that you feel inside of you. In my case, it helped my stronger sensitivity before competitions. It is as if everything moves in diluted time in which the present is the only existing dimension and you are much more receptive.

The competition was approaching. It was time to warm up, my costume was hanging in the locker room; a wonderful dress that once worn, would have let me truly become the gypsy character. Carmen is a seductive and intriguing woman to the point that she disturbs the heart of every person she meets and changes them. Don José goes crazy and kills her, not being able to handle her. In my choreographies I've always wanted to represent femininity in its different aspects. I believe in the feminine energy that I consider magical, pure and delicate but, at the same time, strong and powerful. To bring the emotions that characterize us women on the rink was a priority and a necessity for me, and Carmen represented the emblem of everything female. A gypsy with a strong character, to whom I felt very close to in many ways. But that day I couldn't get "into" her. It was time to compete but where was I? I didn't have the best trial and I wasn't satisfied.

Before entering the rink, Sandro, my choreographer, asked:

"What's up, Paola?"

"I can't get into it. I'm not getting into character."

"That's not true, you're there! Remember who she is: a gypsy who seduces everyone, even just on sight. She is a determined woman in her choices, she takes them to the end, until death, she loves others but wants to keep her freedom and her independence anyway. You are like that too... Think about it!"

I began to recognize myself in the character and feel more connected to her.

"Now you're in it, I see it! The judges are Don José, seduce them!"

Then, it was up to me. A moment before I entered the rink, my mother grabbed my hand and told me: "Between Paola and Carmen, Carmen must win." Only then I realized that Paola and Carmen had to become the same person, the same character. "I am Carmen!" I repeated to myself while I was on the rink... The moment had arrived. Often I immerse myself so much in what I am doing that I enter a trance-like state. It was the same experience I'd had in the Italian Championship: I arrived at the end of my performance basically almost without realizing it. For the first time, I received a perfect 10 even in the technical

120

score. Once more the magic of the competition had taken shape, once more I had removed the mask of my daily life to bring out a completely new Paola, a Paola that manifests only in this way.

This happens to me because I feel that, in that moment, there are no judgments, no sense of fault, nor frustration. Entering the rink is a liberation, a way to bring out my true personality. I carry my life there, freed from the superfluous and I find my pure essence.

When the competition ended, a lady saw me at the cafe and said to me: "You are so small in person, but on the rink you look so big!" It was one of the best compliments I could ever receive. To get on the rink and create magic, to become "larger than life," both for myself and for those watching me, is an opportunity I have at my disposal. That opportunity is a gift that I must take advantage of. Each one of us has our own talent and we must have the courage to recognize it and above all, share it with others.

After the award ceremony my mother came to me smiling and said: "Paola, I can tell you now. Before the competition I dreamt of your grandmother telling me: the one who enters sixth in the competition, wins." I was shaking, the sixth entrant had been me.

Chapter 7
2013 Trust Yourself

2012 had been a turning point for me in both sports and life. I was really grateful for what I had accomplished. My relationship with Marco was proceeding very well and I went to live with him. But a question always echoed in my mind: "What do I want to do after competing?"

I was working as a physical therapist, teaching Pilates, coaching in my skating club, I created choreographies, trained and danced. I knew I couldn't skate forever even if it was what gave me the most joy. But I was twenty-nine years old. How long could I continue to compete? I decided to talk to the doctor who asked me in turn:

"What do you really want to do when you grow up?"

This question again.

"I don't know doctor, if I think of my life without being able to express myself on the skating rink, I feel empty. I know that sooner or later I will have to stop, but I'm afraid. I've come so far with all my strength, it seems that I have fought so many battles to conquer the world's titles. It's like skating is a child for me, I can't abandon it..."

"Don't abandon it." She answered calmly. "You're not ready to let go of this part of your life and that's okay. In any case, remember that what you have built will remain a part of you forever. Don't see it as an aspect to be eliminated. Although I really believe that you must continue, your mission isn't finished."

I felt at peace, because her words described my mood exactly.

"It's true doctor. I'd love to continue to skate forever but why can't I? In another life I would have liked to be a musician so I could go on until I die!" I answered laughing.

"I know Paola," she was laughing too, "You'll see that you will find a way to express yourself in harmony with the different needs of all ages. Have trust, the universe only wants the best for you."

She was right. "Trust" was the key word. We need to develop confidence in ourselves and in something bigger than us that's there to take care of us. My attention, at that point, moved to another question: after Carmen, what other choreography would be good enough? I had put my heart and soul into bringing it to the stage and had received great success. How would I find another one, different but just as involving?

Sandro Guerra, my choreographer, proposed the Can-Can. Initially, I was skeptical about it. It seemed trivial and to be honest, even a little childlike compared to Carmen. But Sandro insisted and I trusted him. I needed new stimuli to improve and a person to guide me from the choreographic point of view. I went to Trieste twice and when the piece took shape, I entered the character.

The Can-Can has to do with women's emancipation. I understood that even if the theme was frivolous and ironic, the role of women in that period was not at all. It was an historic moment of revolution and self-affirmation. It was scandalous to uncover ankles, let alone the back part! The name Can-Can derives from *Scandal-Scandal*, the title of a newspaper article appeared after one of the first dance performances. The doctor advised me to take this character to a higher level, inviting me to take inspiration from Geishas. Knowing that the World Championships would be held in Asia, she suggested that I bring an Oriental touch to the rink. Geishas are extremely cultured and refined women who nourish their seductive power. Learning to communicate this with body language and dance, they develop a great dialogic ability.

They dedicate their lives to the cultivating this art and become very elegant and delicate. Female seduction is closely related to deep self-awareness. The sense of feminine power is very much at the heart of my beliefs and I made sure to emphasize it in my choreography. During the training, I was very much into the part. The idea of paying close attention to every single aspect fascinated me particularly, especially the movements of my hands. I don't know to what extent the work of identification with the character and the background both emerged on the rink, but I was perfectly in the role: a cultured Can-Can dancer and an ironic and seductive artist.

To embody a character with a different story every year, stimulates profound aspects of my personality that sometimes I'm not even aware of. On the rink, I wanted to be sparkling, cheerful, ironic and above all to transmit positive energy to the audience.

Becoming aware of what you want to communicate is the real key. I believe the public always needs to perceive what the artist is doing to be able to feel the same. When I finished the choreography we were already at mid-June, and less than a month later I was going to compete at the Italian Championships. I couldn't wait to compete. It went very well and I won the title! Everyone liked the Can-Can!

I was particularly happy because I had felt a huge sense of satisfaction during the course of the competition and I wanted to experience the same inner state at the World Championships in Taipei at the beginning of November. The preparation was quite intense, but everything went well. The doctor helped to keep me self-aware and present in each moment. One day I went to her and she arrived with raisins...

"Take them Paola, I brought them for you!"

"Thanks, I'll just take a couple because I'm not too crazy about raisins."

Without thinking too much I took the raisins and I put them in my mouth. The doctor was watching me.

"How much attention have you put into doing that?"

"Do you mean in taking the raisins and eating them?"

"Yes!"

"Not much, I guess I did it rather automatically."

"I've noticed!" She said smiling. "Now repeat the same thing but listen, feel, taste and experience more closely what you are doing in the moment. Immerse yourself in the present. Take the raisins, touch them. What feeling do they give you on your fingers? Close your eyes, smell them, bring them to your mouth and calmly taste them, savor and enjoy the moment."

I didn't fully understand what the message was but, as always, I trusted her and repeated my action with a totally different approach.

"It's a whole different experience!" I told her with a state of calm and awareness that I perceived in every part of my body.

"I agree. You've got it. How many times in life do we really live in the present?"

When I became aware of it, I was impressed to think of so many moments in my days when I didn't experience myself fully because my attention was on the future or in the past: riding my bike, while eating, while shopping, while I was brushing my teeth...

"But it's so difficult to live like this." I replied.

"It's hard because we're not used to it, and I'm not asking you to change everything completely in one day. Begin to simply pay attention to the present at some point during each day. When you're distracted and thinking about something else, come back to the present. Your brain will clear itself from the distraction and focus on the present moment. Focus in on a meditative state in which you are there, alive, in union with yourself and with the world. So, it makes no sense to fear what has still to take place, or to be negatively influenced by past experiences. Thanks to these experiences you grew up. If what has intimidated you in the past happens again, you would probably react differently. The only thing you can do is to stay in the present and live in the gift of the here and now, so you will never be afraid again."

"It's true but I'm not used to that at all. In general, I'm projected on the future or focused on the past. How many times do I forget that I'm living in here and now? What can help me to remember?"

"Breathe," she replied to me calmly. "Whenever you get lost, stop and listen to your breath. It is one of the most powerful things we possess. Take three breaks in the day and take ten breaths. Imagine taking in the energy from the universe, from the galaxy and stars, and to exhale negativity, tiredness and frustration. Let go of what doesn't help you and recharge yourself with positive energy. Try it now: close your eyes and breathe in the way I just described."

I felt divine after the exercise. Why did I never take a minute to listen to myself?

"Thanks doctor. But how can I apply this to sports?"

She smiled. "I knew you would ask me this question. You see, when you train, or you're in the competition, you have to be totally in the present, alive in the moment, be fully there. Try listening to your body while you dance, feel your breath and the music that accompanies you. Being in the present means that if something happens, you're ready to turn the page and restore a clear state of mind to start again. How many athletes get stuck when they make a mistake and aren't able to recover? This happens because their mind is anchored to their past error and it fails to flow into the present."

I nodded in agreement, willing her to go on. That did happen to me quite often.

"It's true, it's not simple to actually live in the here and now, without worries or regrets, but it's the only thing we can do. Thanks for the advice doctor, I will put it into practice immediately. I'm leaving next week for the World Championships, so I don't think we'll see each other until I'm back!"

"I'm sure everything will be fine Paola," she said, hugging me. "I see you already there, on the roof of the world. Go and shine like the brightest star in the galaxy!"

"I'll do my best!" I answered with a smile, feeling tears coming to my eyes.

It was time to leave for Taipei. I was calm, I visualized the future but I lived in the present with the help of my breath. And this taught me a crucial point:

When you visualize the future, never lose awareness
of being in the here and now.
Your breath allows you to restore mental clarity
and presence and helps you to better fixate
on the moment.

The trip to Taipei went well. I tried to rest as much as I could. Preparation for the World Championship involves so much stress and the only thing I could do was to recover my energy during the flight. My mother, my brother Matteo and Marco were joining me the following day. I was so happy to have them by my side, especially my brother who couldn't be there the year before. With him I have a special relationship, it's almost as if we are twins, despite the five years between us. I have always experienced a profound connection with him, an energy and tranquility at the same time. He represents happiness for me and being able to have him by my side in the course of the competition, meant I could count on his huge support.

When I entered the arena I was a little disappointed: it was small and I felt its energy was a bit off, but I tried not to be influenced by these thoughts. The most important thing was that the surface of the rink was good. The night before the competition I slept very well, despite the time difference. The trial in the morning went well but my tension rose because I felt a strong external pressure. Not everyone wanted me to win. The environment is sometimes hostile and circumstances can really interfere with one's performance. On that occasion more than ever, I had to contend with the competition and with the envy of other people. Seeing me in crisis, my mother took me aside and said: "Paola, shake all these harmful thoughts off. Stay focused on what you can do and do not waste energy listening to others."

I nodded and replied: "I know, I'm here trying hard, but all of this hurts. I want to start the competition as soon as possible. The most difficult step for me is the first compulsory dance and as you know, once that's over everything else is easy." My mom took my hands in hers and told me: "Remember who you are and what you're worth, do not allow others to break you down with meaningless talk. Isolate from everything and everyone. Only think of yourself and take out that grit, as you've always done."

I smiled and hugged her tightly. My mother always manages to tell me the right things at the right times.

When someone challenges you, do not give up, get involved
and show them who you are. In sports you also need this.
Outside we are all friends, but on the rink you fight,
and the moment you decide to fight,
you must be there entirely with honesty.

I was ready to enter the competition, I couldn't wait. The waltz that worried me so much went well and the fox-trot even better. I had a regular competition, I was occupying the first position with five judges in favor out of seven. I was satisfied, but as always, after the compulsory dances, I did not allow myself to rejoice because the competition was in full swing.

The adrenaline remained in the air until the night. I took a bit of melatonin to relax and go to sleep, but nothing happened. The hours passed and I stayed awake. The muscles in my legs were sore and I needed to rest to be able to compete. At 5:00 AM, after turning over and over again in bed relentlessly, I got up, I filled the tub with hot water and stood still there for an hour. I went back to bed hoping to be more relaxed, but still nothing. I gave up, I got up and went to have breakfast. I had a headache and a crazy pain in my muscles, but an athlete has to compete in any condition, pains and discomfort are not allowed. Somehow, you just always have to go out there and do it.

I did the free dance trial well, despite everything. When I finished, I went to the locker room and a coach of the national team came to me and said: "Paola, you're not doing the stop before the sequence of steps for the straight line. You know it's mandatory, right?"

This caught me in surprise. "How great is it to learn about something like this when you don't have any more trials and the only thing to do is to change the steps during the competition!" I thought. There were two sequences of mandatory steps: one diagonally and one in a straight line. It wasn't clear from the regulation if it was necessary to make one stop before the line or if it was enough to mark the beginning of the sequence with a movement. I called my mother to tell her what I had just been told. I remembered that she had doubts during a training session in Genoa, so we tried to reverse the diagonal steps with the straight line. We had asked several competent people for confirmation as the regulation was not so specific.

They had answered that what I was doing was correct: a movement to mark the beginning of the line without necessarily having to stop. We trusted this and hadn't made any changes. But now the rumor that I didn't have a stop before the line had spread and I would have risked a penalty. It seemed strange to me that a lot of coaches and judges had seen my choreography both at the meeting before Worlds, and during the trials in those days, and no one had said anything until the moment I didn't have any more chances to change my routine.

"We did have that doubt, Paola!" My mother told me, "Remember the change we tried that time? You must do that tonight. Now I'm going to see if we can manage to have a few minutes on another rink, so you can try it at least once."

I looked at her nodding but I was confused.

I managed to get five minutes on a training rink and I tried to change the choreography. This meant adding new steps and directions. It was yet another challenge to face.

"Why is it never easy, mom?"

"I'm sorry about this, believe me, but you will pull out even more grit and determination. When you have to face a challenge you win. Don't worry, I'm sure you'll make it even better."

My mother was right, it was time to stay focused and not get caught up in panic. I went to the nearby rink to try the change. It seemed to work well with the music. Having done this little trial run really reassured me.

The tiredness of the night, however, began to be unbearable and I had to go back to the hotel. I threw myself on the bed, collapsing into a deep sleep. I dreamed that my grandmother came to get me in her car to take me for a ride. I woke up and smiled because my angel was once again with me to protect me.

It was time to get ready and go to the rink for the competition.

I was nervous about the change I had to deal with, but I trusted myself: it was a good challenge to overcome.

I asked my mom to tie the corset of my dress for the Can-Can and I really felt like a dancer that was preparing to go on stage. I started the warm up.

As I ran, I breathed deeply and repeated to myself: "I can do it!" I visualized the change that I had to do and I tried it during the warm-up. I went into the audience to get a hug from Marco and my brother, then I put on the skates following the sequence of rituals. We were almost there. I looked at myself once again in the mirror to put on my makeup and, with a determined sigh I told myself: "Go Paola it's time to give them a show!"

I felt that my mother was a little nervous about the change of choreography but she wasn't showing it: "Remember to have fun! You and the music, nothing else!"

I entered the rink with an immense determination, remembering what I wanted to communicate to the public. During the program I tried to be present, as the doctor had told me, to live moment by moment, remaining focused on the changes to do. I reassured myself of that exactly halfway through the competition.

The audience was very involved, accompanying the dance by clapping their hands. It went very well from beginning to end and I finished the program in a split with my arms in the air. I slapped the floor of the rink with my hand and exclaimed: "I did it!" The audience gave me a standing ovation and I was in a state of ecstasy!

Leaving the rink, I greeted my grandfather, in heaven. He had asked me to wave to him at the end of every program and I have always dedicated this final moment to him. The previous year he got up at 4:00 AM to see my competition streaming in Auckland. This time he had looked at me from above, next to my grandmother.

I hugged my mom. The score was high, some 10s in artistic expression, once again on the screen, *Place 1*!

Every year has been different and full of different emotions that have always put me under test.

They say that winning is a habit, as it is to lose. As for me, more than getting used to victory, I had cultivated a winning inner attitude.

If you think you could fail and you give up at the first challenge,
it will be difficult to get a good result.

Remember, there are three main ingredients for achieving success: grit, determination and courage.

Grit is the motivation that drives you to achieve a result, it is the fire that lights you up, it's your passion.

Determination is the perseverance that allows you to

work hard, not just for a week or for a month but over the years, constantly, to make your dream a reality.

Finally, courage comes from the Latin Cor, which means heart. It is acting with trust, despite the fears and insecurities, to look beyond the obstacle and exit the comfort zone.

On that occasion, these three virtues had allowed me to reach my goal with my heart.

When the competition ended, people began to ask me: "Now that you have won the fifth World Championship will you stop, right?" Or jokingly, "Now that you have filled a whole hand, will you want to fill the other one too?!" These questions bothered me. They caused a feeling of discomfort and I didn't know how to answer. I felt that there was envy and I didn't like it.

To quit skating would have created an unbridgeable gap within me and I didn't know if I would ever be ready. After the award ceremony I went to the lobby of the building and I saw the Reus 2014 World Championships logo. I stopped and said to myself:

"I want to be there!"

There will always be envious people who will do anything to throw you down and make you feel that you're not worth it. But there is a remarkable difference between the Champion and the Commentator: The Champion Achieves the Results, The Commentator Doesn't.

Chapter 8

2014 Put Love
in Everything You Do

I was almost thirty years old and I felt that I didn't have much time left. With five World Championship titles in a row, what more could I aspire to? What could motivate me to go forward? I wanted to continue but I was afraid to be repetitive in my life. I talked about it with my mom, my brother, my dad, my choreographer, the doctor, Max, Marco and my friends.

The answer was always the same: "Do what you feel. However, remember that once you stop it will be difficult to compete again."

I was scared. I still couldn't let go. It seemed a shame to throw away something that had cost me so much effort, and above all, quitting skating would mean I'd have to stop truly expressing myself. I continued to train whilst the inner debate rattled my inner peace.

One day, taken by despair, I gave myself an ultimatum. I had to decide. I took my training diary and I started to throw down these thoughts:

You have wondered for too long whether to continue or not, you have to make a decision by really listening to your heart and not what others say! Why can't you stop? Are you afraid of losing? And if you lose, what would happen? Or, if you're afraid of the future, what will happen without being able to express yourself? Are you really ready for that emptiness?

Otherwise continue, do not give victory to those who want you to stop. It's time to step up and be in the game again. There's nothing bad about continuing, you are not weak because of it. Hold your life in your hands and drive it to your next target. Go ahead with determination because the mental limits that are put upon you are nothing but the crystallization of your fears.

After this outburst I realized that I wanted to continue and I would end my career with the World Championships in Reus. Once the decision was made, the inner storm had finally calmed down. Even the training was going better. I had gotten back on track.

When we have to decide between something, we always have two choices available: love and fear. I had chosen once again the love for this sport. I was aware of the fact that I should have brought a totally different program compared to the previous year, definitely one more technical. Sandro proposed an interpretation of Mary Poppins. Among all of the Walt Disney films, Mary Poppins has always been my favorite. As a child, I used to watch it every morning and I knew every line by heart.

Everything is Possible Even the Impossible.

The music was known to the public and for the fiftieth anniversary of the film, *Saving Mr. Banks* had just come out. There were so many reasons in favor of that program.

The doctor had suggested a great and powerful picture to me: "Just as she finally flies away and leaves all of the good she has done, you'll do the same and you'll be ready to turn to new horizons!"

I really liked the idea of leaving my place after having accomplished my mission and flying to other goals to contribute elsewhere. I started working on it. Then, Sandro called me.

"Paola I have some new music for you to listen to, it's a baroque flamenco. I think you could interpret it very well. I'll send it to you. Let me know what you think!"

I listened to it and it was a very beautiful piece... But what about Mary Poppins? She was my childhood idol and I had already started to create my performance piece in my mind. I went to Trieste to start the choreography. We listened to both pieces of music together at the rink and at the end we decided to go for the flamenco. The music was totally different from the year before and it fitted very well with a technically difficult program. The piece took shape in a short amount of time.

The execution was complex but it didn't scare me. I was ready to train hard to make it smooth and impactful. As always, visualization helped me since the time available before the Italian Championship was running out.

During the competition, the external pressure I felt the year before was gone. Instead, I was overcome with a feeling of great support... and I saw sincere admiration in the eyes of others.

Perhaps, having decided that it would be my last year competing, my attitude towards the competition and the people were different.

Eventually what happens is nothing but the mirror
of what we have inside.

The compulsory dances scheduled for that year, the pasodoble and the tango, were congenial to me and the performances went very well. I was in first position and there was a good gap between me and the skater in second place. Before the free dance, I continued to visualize my performance with the music and, I couldn't understand why, but at the end of the diagonal steps, I envisioned a small gap of two seconds. It was as if the song was "skipping" for a moment. However, I didn't pay too much attention to this issue because I was eager to compete.

I did my hair and makeup with care yet quickly. Generally, this for me, is a good sign for the competition. I entered last, exactly as when I had performed Carmen, and I felt the same sensations as I had two years before. Coincidentally, the score was also the same: 9.7 in technical content and a perfect 10 in the artistic content. I also won the Italian Championship of 2014. I had done an excellent performance, apart from a small indecision at the end of the diagonal part, exactly where I'd imagined that empty space during the visualization. Without knowing it, I'd trained the mistake into my mind.

It's important to pay close attention when doing visualizations because the brain records everything, mistakes included. From that day, I fully realized that visualization is a really powerful tool that, if not used in the correct way, can give life to negative performances. The doctor had warned me from the beginning: when you see an error or a blank space, it's important to find out what its meaning is, rewind the tape and start over again until everything starts to flow the right way.

When the competition ended, I went to the locker room to grab my phone and bag and I immediately realized that something was missing: my wallet! I couldn't believe it! I looked everywhere for it, but it was gone. Someone had stolen it. The joy and excitement were immediately reset to bitterness and disbelief at the theft. It must have been stolen by someone who knew me and knew that I kept my bag there because only athletes and coaches could enter the changing room. Why would someone do something so bad and ruin what was such an incredible moment for me? The act had left me speechless. In the evening, instead of celebrating, I went to the police, miserable about what had happened. Regardless, during the awards ceremony, I tried not to think about it and just enjoy that special moment knowing that it would be the last time I was in an Italian Championship. I shook hands with all of the athletes who had shared the journey with me for so many years.

Leave a Trace - World Championships 2014

I spent the summer quietly, mostly in the mountains walking and breathing in clean, fresh air. For me, Chamois is the ideal place to recover energy. I get to be in contact with nature, I can sleep and the rhythms of my life slow down. With a lucid and calm mind, I could face the World Championship in the best way.

I wanted to live the last competition with joy, awareness and maturity... So I talked with the doctor.

"Why do you skate Paola?" She asked me.

"Because I couldn't live without it!" I replied sincerely.

"What is skating for you? What does it represent?"

"For me, skating is art. It's the expression of my full

self. I put my soul into every performance. It's my way of freeing myself from the boundaries and limits of life."

"You know what? I want you to take the mental techniques further this time. I want you to have a greater and more open vision of what you are doing. Mental techniques help you, but in this competition, I want you to really use love and passion with them to truly communicate to the audience what you are feeling. Try to visualize what you are doing on a more spiritual level. It is your soul that dances, that shines out the light of love, and even the last spectator sitting at the very top of the stairs will have to feel it. Yes Paola, you will have to emanate an energy of love. This will be the key to your success!"

"Nice doctor! I want people to remember my dance and the love that I have always put into skating. For me, it's a goodbye and it's really important that I leave a trace of myself behind."

She took my hands and went on: "You will stay forever in the history of this sport. You are a star that shines in the sky and you will be an example for future generations. No one will forget your energy."

Sometimes, taken by the frenzy and the routine, we forget that we are actually spiritual beings.

We are on Earth for a bigger reason.

Each one of us is here to evolve in life and complete a personal mission.

I have always felt that through my art, I could bring beauty to the world.

After this conversation with the doctor, I felt deeply connected to the universe, as if something bigger supported me and took my hands leading me towards my goal. I left her office in this wonderful mood.

At Reus, in Spain, everything was great from the start.

The rink was in good condition and the trials went very well right from the beginning.

As always, my mom, Matteo and Marco joined me. This time, some athletes and parents of our team came too. Support was not lacking and a lot of people, once again, followed me from home on the live stream.

During the competition, I am always in this state of high consciousness, where everything happens more quickly. I am more receptive. It's as if I'm vibrating on another frequency and the informations arrive at a higher speed.

Perhaps it has happened to you that you think of someone and shortly after you meet this person? Or that you want something and then it seemingly magically appears to you? So, before a competition, many signs often speak to me and it seems that I succeed in attracting the right situations with my thoughts. I remember that during the warm up I was thirsty and I thought: "I'd like a little water now." I turned around and there was a new bottle, still unopened, on the floor!

The World Championship began with the pasodoble. I entered and was very concentrated. I had a new pink and black dress which I liked immensely and totally helped me become the character. Despite this, it was the dance that scared me the most. But it went wonderfully and even the score was high! There was a big time gap between the two dances, which I don't like at all, but I was quite calm because I was very good at the tango. A different sign, however, frightened me.

A moment before entering, my mother turned to me: "Come on Paola! Give me ten, I want to feel your energy!"

I hit my hands firmly against hers and my bracelet, which I put on her wrist, opened and fell to the ground. I felt something clutching my chest and, I don't know why, but I interpreted it as a negative sign. I didn't want to think about it so I entered the rink focused on my tango.

Everything was going well when, at the end of the first lap, I felt my right foot slip away, my left leg went down and in a fraction of a second I almost found myself on the ground! There was a roar in the building. I don't know how I managed to pull myself up and resume the dance. I felt myself dying inside, I couldn't believe it had really happened. I managed to save the situation but the error was still there.

I finished the second lap virtually on auto-pilot and I remembered the words of the doctor: "Stay in the present, whatever happens, turn the page and go forward." So I did, I finished the dance well but I was embittered. Why the tango?! I came out of the rink with my eyes burning, holding back tears. I didn't understand how it was possible. The score was good, and despite everything I was in first position, but it was like having received a slap in the face and I was struggling to recover. Everyone comforted and complimented me for my rescue but I couldn't give it a reason, I couldn't understand why it had happened.

I went back to the hotel without talking to anyone. I was really hit by the incident and I truly had not expected it. I hardly slept, I couldn't move past the error I had committed. The next morning, I arrived at the rink in confusion and when it was time to try the free dance, I changed all of the wheels on my skates fearing that I would slip again. The training went well, but the fear from the night before was still inside of me. Throughout the whole day I only managed to drink a little bit of juice. My stomach was in knots. I struggled to "turn the page."

Between the trial and the competition, I went back to the hotel to rest. I locked myself in the bathroom and took a cold shower to wake up from the mental torpor. I tried to breathe and remember everything I had learned over the years.

I reminisced about the previous World Championships. I rewatched my videos and I thought about how many personal battles I had won.

This was the last competition of my career and it was time to fight, not to surrender. I remembered my goal: to bring love to the rink and to communicate that to the audience. I tried to visualize the heat and the light in my heart and to recharge by inhaling sunlight.

I imagined that the energy of the galaxy was coming into me and, in the meantime, I repeated to myself: "I can do it, I am love!" This is a very powerful exercise that puts me in contact with the deepest part of me, entering into a direct connection with my soul.

In the end, I spoke these words: "Grandparents, from up there, take care of me. I feel I need your support one more time. Thank you!"

A warrior does not give up what he loves.
He finds the love in what he does.

A warrior is not about perfection or victory or invulnerability.
He is about absolute vulnerability.

That's the only true courage.

Dan Millman

I went to the rink. On the bus, I had been talking with a coach about the fact that it would be the last competition I took part in and I started to tell him about my plans for the future. Talking about them helped me to calm down and understand that skating couldn't be the pin to spin my whole existence around.

Once at the rink, I got ready. I tried out my routine without skates, with the music in my earphones and I tried to isolate myself. But I still felt a sense of inner instability. My mother, seeing me acting so strangely, asked me: "What's going on Paola?"

"I can't wait to finish!" I had never felt this way, wanting to finish as soon as possible but I couldn't handle the tension.

"I want to do well mom! I want to close the circle in the best way but I'm afraid of making mistakes like last night. I can't afford it, I risk losing the title."

"You know that the more you tell yourself you have to do well, the worse it will be for you. The best performances come when you enjoy yourself in the moment and do not think too much. When you follow the flow of the music and completely immerse yourself in your bubble where there is only you, that's when you win!"

She was right, I took two minutes to breathe deeply and then I began my usual rituals. I put a butterfly-shaped clip in my hair, I finished my makeup and I tied my skates in the same way as usual. I was ready for the competition. The tension was high, but I knew that I had to do my part on the rink and communicate to the audience what I was feeling inside.

Before entering, my mother squeezed my hands and, following our ritual, she said: "Go Paola, have fun!" I entered smiling and repeated: "Go Paola, have fun!"

Waiting for the music, I could see my brother with the whole group of fans who had come from Genoa to support me. I stared at them and could feel an exchange of a very deep energy. They were there for me.

I started the flamenco with incredible strength inside and tried to communicate all the love and joy that I felt. I wanted every dance step to leave a part of myself inside the hearts of every spectator. Everything happened quickly. In the last thirty seconds I realized that I was almost done and I put even more energy into what I was doing. I ended with the crowd's roar and a personal sense of immense gratitude! I looked at the sky and thanked my grandparents and then thanked the audience who had supported me throughout the competition. At the edge of the rink, my mother squeezed me, saying: "Whatever happens I want you to know that you will always remain in people's hearts. I am proud of you!"

I went into the audience to watch the conclusion of the competition with my whole group of Italian friends. When the last athlete finished, the ranking came out on the screen.

For the sixth time in a row I had finished first! My mother ran over to hug me and with shining eyes told me: "You did it again! Thanks Paola!"

"Thanks to you for always being by my side and for taking me to the highest step of the podium even today."

Since childhood, my mother, besides being a mom, has prepared and guided me to get to where I am today, and for this I will always be grateful.

After the awards, they interviewed me and I immediately said that I would stop skating. I needed to announce it, to give it a reason. If they were asking me why, I was answering: "There is a time to receive and a time to give, I want to step on to the other side where I can share my experience with someone else."

It was really time to pass on the baton even though I knew it would be tough. Behind the result, there is always a huge load of work, both mental and physical. In those six years I had fought with all of myself to always be on top and I had done it with all of my heart. I had given so much and received just as much, but I still felt a sense of emptiness. That World Championship had really put me to the test.

In the evening, I wrote a post on Facebook announcing my retirement to everyone. I wrote it with tears in my eyes. It was necessary to close that door and look forward to a still poorly outlined future.

I would have coached and especially choreographed, which I'm particularly passionate about, but I knew that probably nothing would have given me the same adrenaline as the competitions. Was I ready to deal with all of that? At that moment I didn't know, but I felt that was the only way to go.

The same night, Genoa was hit by a torrential flood. The water also flooded into the skating rink and into the changing rooms destroying everything that was found inside. I don't know why, but I have always associated this natural disaster with the end of my career.

My mother and my brother came home the day after my competition. I remained until the end of the championships trying to soak up the atmosphere.

During the journey home on the bus, I began to write articles for my blog. The mental training of those years had to be shared with other athletes.

When I saw my rink in Genoa, however, I was shocked. The flood had caused serious damage but it was the only place where the athletes of my team could train. While I was drying the floor, a deep sense of sadness arose in me. "How is it possible that after six World titles I'm here just drying the floor of my rink and my athletes cannot train?" I wondered: "Why does no one care? What more should I do?"

I felt a sense of impotence, and regarding this, I still feel it today. Being able to have a big indoor skating rink as a place to practice a sport could be the basis for building a future for some of the young people here.

Through sports, children grow up, have fun, stay healthy and avoid wrong friendships. I really believe that sports are a school of life and we should invest more in centers and in the technical and psychological training of the instructors, especially in the youngsters who will be our future.

Chapter 9

2015 Let Go

I didn't organize a party for the World Championship and the end of my career. I didn't think there was anything to celebrate. I immediately threw myself into new projects. I needed to turn my attention somewhere else. My blog, called *PaolAttitude* from www.paolafraschini. com, took off. It was a totally new activity for me. I started to draw t-shirts and training diaries. I worked really hard to create new and original choreographies and I also enrolled in a musical course and contemporary dance in the evening, and I was attending yoga in the morning. These new outlets gave me the energy to organize my life again without the competitions.

I traveled with Marco to South America. He helped me with the creation and editing of videos and the production of *PaolAttitude*. He was in a bit of a crisis with his job. He had a permanent position in a company in Genoa, but the office administration tasks were not exactly suited to his charismatic personality. His strong social skills and interest in other languages and cultures made him feel like he was in a cage. He used to come home exhausted every night. Seeing him like that hurt me. I had the same experiences with physical therapy and understood how working a job that you don't like, feels like carrying a cross on your back every day.

Most of us spend at least eight hours a day working, which is a third of our day. Considering that an additional eight hours or so we spend sleeping, we are left to live with very little time. It is so important to do a job that gives us satisfaction and excites us because of this.

I enrolled in physical therapy because at that time it seemed more important to have a permanent job rather than risk things with an unstable job, even if it was more in line with my passions. In Italy this belief is very deeply rooted especially in the generation before mine. You can easily fall into the trap of the "permanent position," giving up aspirations, or even just the need for satisfaction. The much sought after "safe job" ends up turning off all the enthusiasm you have and, little by little, disconnects us from ourselves.

When I was doing the internship at the hospital, I saw so many employees looking at the clock, complaining and doing the minimum necessary. I thought it was normal that work was a duty and not a pleasure. Until the time that I realized it could also be the contrary.

I believe instead that the universe helps those who are brave and choose to transform their own passion into a job, running the risk of trying to be happier.

Slowly I left physical therapy, giving space to the things that gave me more satisfaction, above all teaching and choreographing. I would have loved to do competitions as a job but, unfortunately, it was not possible.

That was how I urged Marco to resign and help me with my new projects. It was not easy at all. He thought about it a lot, and then with an act of courage, he did it.

A while later he fell into a sort of depression. He

couldn't sleep at night and he couldn't find any direction in his life. But this moment of darkness had served to shake off everything that was no longer a part of him and set him off on what would be his new path.

To be unemployed, especially for a man, I think, is one of the hardest things to bear.

In May, we spent three days in Ibiza and over there he found old friends who offered him work in the summer organizing island tours by jeep. I saw a glimmer of light in his eyes. He had worked in Ibiza years ago and was in love with that island. So I encouraged him to go. This meant that we'd be apart, but I felt that it was the only thing to do for his good.

So it was, at the end of May he left and I stayed in Genoa to carry on with my work.

I had supported him with all of my strength but I didn't realize that at that point, I was rather weak too. Skating had been part of my life forever. Training and competing made me feel alive. To stop, change habits and look for a new road, took energy away from me. I was exhausted. I had held hard for months, trying to keep calm and to find new reasons for living, but when he left, I collapsed. I had a high fever for two days and I could do nothing but sleep.

They were intense months, above all emotionally. Without Marco and skating, I felt lost. Furthermore, all the athletes at my skating club were training for the Italian Championships scheduled in less than two months. Seeing the others train, and not being part of the competition anymore hurt. It was as if my soul was imprisoned. That was how I started skating and training again.

What I was doing didn't make sense but I was clinging onto something known to make me feel more secure.

I was afraid of the future and, above all, I feared I couldn't find anything that made me feel as good as skating. At that time, I spoke with many people and everyone told me that competing again wouldn't be beneficial for my personal growth. I understood it but I couldn't cut that umbilical cord.

That year I attended a course with Max Gentile, with whom I did some very deep work on myself. I was mainly focused on my life's direction to really understand where to channel my energy. I met him for a personal interview and talked to him openly about how I felt.

"Max, I learned a lot during your course. I entered into a deeper connection with myself, but now I have come to a point where I need to make some bigger decisions and I'm afraid."

"Of course, I understand. Every choice brings a renunciation of something else. I know how important skating is for you and it's normal that you're frightened to leave your world. I know what a great commitment you had to make, the sacrifices you made to get where you are today, but it is also true that you cannot continue forever. At some point you have to make a decision."

I fully agreed with him but I knew that if I took that step I would suffer and I didn't want to.

"You know, I like to teach but it's not my ambition. I would like to continue skating in another environment and make a living developing shows. For years I've been wanting to bring skating out of the rinks and competitions, but I don't know how to do it."

"I know, it's been a while since you told me. Let's visualize your future and see what it reveals."

I couldn't help but trust him. In that situation I clung to any answer or sign that could arrive. Through breathing, he led me to a state of very deep relaxation.

152

"Ok Paola, try to imagine yourself in a month and tell me where you are."

"In Ibiza, but I see it tarnished. I'm not well. I feel strange."

I took a long pause in silence because I didn't know what to say.

"Let's try to go further in time, in three months, tell me what you see!"

At first, I couldn't visualize anything, but slowly, the blurred image of myself, while skating, appeared at the bottom of the screen.

"Max I don't know why but it's not clear to me. I feel empty."

"Don't worry. If you think of yourself competing what do you feel?"

"I see myself on a small rink. I feel like I don't have space, like I can't give more of myself. I feel tight and I need to escape." I said with a sense of suffocation.

"Let's do this: imagine an indeterminate future, without defining exactly one moment. Can you see something?"

I took a deep breath, calmed down and an image of myself on skates with lights and loud music began to pass through my mind.

"I'm on a stage, I see the audience and I hear the applause. There are other artists but no skaters. I'm good, I can express myself and I finally feel like I'm in my zone."

"Try to fixate on this image in your mind. Listen to what you feel and remember it. It will be very important to direct energy onto the right path. When you're ready, take a deep breath and open your eyes." He smiled and went on: "The stage will be your future, it's there that you'll have to focus on. With the same sensations that you felt today, repeat this vision daily and each time, try to amplify more and more of what you feel. Also, build a physical collage of your dreams. If you see an image that represents the future you want: in magazines, books, newspapers, or posters, cut it out and glue them on a large piece of poster-board that you place somewhere clearly visible in your house. If you don't find images, simply draw them. It is a really powerful exercise. Through the images you will attract what you really want. It is not magic, it works."

I wasn't completely lucid yet but I replied: "I don't know how I'll get there, but I trust the universe will take care of me once again."

"Absolutely. Visualize it as if you've already got what you want, connecting with your center. Reserve ten minutes every day to channel these energies and you will see that you will begin to attract the change that you desire. Have faith in it."

"I will do it Max. But, in your opinion, does it make any sense for me to continue to compete?" I insisted on looking for more confirmations.

"If you want to make a change in your life, you must find the courage to let go of the past. Remember that for new things to enter, you need space. You can't fly out of the nest with weights on your shoulders." This sentence had enlightened me. I had understood that it was time to clean up my life, to let the fresh air come in and sweep away all that didn't belong to me anymore.

"I know it's hard. It's easy to say but hard to do. Life is like that, you always have to get involved and reinvent yourself to discover what comes next. It can't rain forever; you will soon see the light of the sun." He ended there.

I was convinced and determined to change my life, despite seeing the fog in front of me. My friend Federica, a dancer, teacher and choreographer, suggested the book

The Artist's Way by Julia Cameron to me. The author explains how to unlock the artist who lives inside all of us. The book led me through a "growth path" via weekly exercises. One of the first exercises suggests this:

> "Every morning wake up half an hour earlier, get up and write three pages about whatever comes into your mind. It must be an uncontrolled river of thoughts. Do not read the pages again immediately and do not let others read them. Put them in a safe place. Ideally seal them in a secret box."

> "Welcome to the morning pages! They will change you. This week, write at the end of the pages your affirmations of positive choices and all of your negative rants, converting the negative cries into positive affirmations."

I decided to follow this path. The book was full of interesting ideas. It would help me to clarify and stay connected with the baby inside of me, the first true artist, aware of herself and her desires since birth.

In everyday life we risk forgetting what we came to do, what we are like, what makes us feel good. The morning pages were a great tool to review everything that I kept inside of myself. I'll quote a few paragraphs of what I wrote because rereading them now is incredible! I would have never expected that these words would become my reality:

> I have decided to spend two days in Chamois in total silence and solitude to have some time for myself. I made the decision not to compete because I need to be open to new frontiers as an artist. I want to continue skating but in a new form which allows me to do it for a longer time

because it's a way to connect with myself and that's why I can't live without it.

I want to create a new artistic identity. My dream would be to work as a figure skater in a high level artistic field where I can have new incentives and grow professionally. I need to realize myself: work, go on tour, be an artist. It's true, my dreams seem ambitious but I've learned to think big and to believe in them. Everyone tells me it will take time, but the immobility of this period is distressing me. I try to take it as a necessary phase for cleaning and reconnecting with my essence.

Please God, I want to give to the world beauty again through my art. If you gave me this talent, make me be able to express it in full. I ask you to give me the strength and energy to achieve this, to find opportunities and situations that allow me to give life to my projects and my dreams. Thank you...

Positive affirmations followed:

- *I make the right connections/meetings at the right times. People appreciate my art and support me.*

- *I find the solutions and the means to succeed in giving the best of myself and take positive actions despite everything that seems to hold me back.*

- *I put myself first, I'm determined and I go towards my dreams with strength and courage.*

- *My creativity is the most divine part of myself. I let it flow inside of me like a river, it will then overflow and be shared with others.*

I also resumed meetings with the doctor who encouraged me:

"Stay connected to the deepest and truest part of yourself and listen to it, it will guide you to your purpose in life. What did you like to do as a child?"

"To dance! Whenever there were cartoons on, I got up and danced to the music in front of my parents. I did my own personal shows. I felt the need to perform and it made me feel great!"

"You have to talk to that little girl inside of you and tell her that it is not over. That passion is still there. She will soon be able to do it again." She smiled and continued: "In your opinion, what is your main artistic talent?"

I thought about it for a moment and answered: "To immerse myself in a character, in the music, and express what I feel. I won World Championships not for my technique, I had to work really hard on that, but because of my charisma on the rink and what I expressed and communicated to others. That's a natural thing for me. As a child, I was spontaneous. Nobody taught me that."

"You know Paola, if I close my eyes, I see you performing at the Metropolitan in New York. I'm absolutely sure you'll go across the ocean to realize yourself."

I managed to sketch a grimace that wanted to be a smile, in a mixture of hope and disbelief. Then I thanked her and, with good intentions, I prepared to go to Ibiza with Marco for a month.

I left for Ibiza with the idea of resting, making space in my mind and gaining some clarity, but when I got there, I felt lost.

Marco worked all day, I was alone. A partially broken bicycle was my only form of transportation and we shared the house with another person that I didn't know. During the day I listened to music, practiced yoga, wrote my "morning pages" and tried to get new ideas for my career.

Despite everything, I was not well at all. I was missing the competitions and I felt empty.

I tried to fill my days but it seemed that each one was purposeless. The doctor said that was normal.

In sports, and even more during competitions, we create endorphins that are a kind of natural drug for our bodies, and when we don't produce them anymore, we crave them. It's a true withdrawal crisis.

"But you're in Ibiza, relax and have fun!" Everyone was telling me.

It was true, I could relax, but at that moment I was in a hurry and needed to take action. It was a real effort for me as I used to always be actively achieving goals one after another. Meanwhile, with Marco things were not going well. I needed a hug, support, but he was overwhelmed and distracted with his new job and was not there for me. I felt neglected and wanted to go home. I came back from Ibiza demoralized. He seemed to no longer understand "us" and this hurt.

I felt distant, we weren't on the same planet. I needed someone to take care of me, but he was elsewhere. I left hoping to recharge with positive energy but I came back even more confused than before. The two columns of my life, Marco on one side, and skating on the other, had collapsed at the same time. When he returned, after the summer, he told me that he had decided to move to Ibiza.

"What do we do about us?" I asked him.

"I don't know." He answered.

That statement was enough for me to understand that our lives no longer shared a common direction.

We left each other to continue down our own roads and pursue separate personal dreams. We had a lot of back and forth, it wasn't easy at all to let him go, but sometimes life decides things for you. I've learned that when we truly love someone, we respect them and their choices and give them the freedom to move on.

At the same time, the World Championships took place in Colombia and a new champion was on the podium instead of me. I felt set aside, and the fear of having made the wrong choices attacked me more and more each day. "Why do I have to give up the things I like and suffer?" I continued to repeat. I really couldn't give a sensible direction to my life. "Maybe I'm doing everything wrong."

There was a song by an Italian singer called Elisa, *"Qualcosa che non c'è,"* (translated: *Something That is Not There)* that I was always listening to those days and the words gave me a strong hope:

> *"And miraculously I haven't stopped dreaming*
> *Miraculously I can't stop to hope*
> *And if there is a secret it's*
> *Do everything as if*
> *You can only see the Sun"*

In the fall, in a moment of inspiration, I said to myself, "It's time for me to do something. I want to collect what I sowed throughout these years. I deserve more than this."

One day, I went on the website for Cirque du Soleil. I was looking at the photos and watching the videos and became incredibly inspired! On the website, there's a casting section where you can upload your profile, resume, photos and videos. On a whim, I decided to create a casting profile for myself and did so with huge momentum, yet in the following days, I almost forgot about it.

> *Do not allow anyone to steal your dreams.*
> *They are the fire that shine light on your path even*
> *in the darkest moments.*

Something was moving in my life. Sandro, my choreographer, called me from Verona to compete in a skating quartet. A girl on the team had quit and they needed a replacement. He had also suggested this collaboration a year earlier, but I had disregarded it because I was in a very confusing state of mind. It would have been really complicated to reconcile training, work and the new projects I had taken on.

I would have had to travel to Verona every week and this required significant mental, physical and financial commitments. I was doubtful, but at that time I really needed to get out of Genoa a little bit and it was an opportunity to skate again. Competing with three other people was also a new experience, so I accepted it.

I went to Verona on a Sunday for a trial. Immediately, there was good chemistry between the four of us.

Happy to work with my choreographer again, I felt I had started this adventure with real enthusiasm and passion. Leaving Genoa also allowed me to see things from another point of view. The train trips gave me time to think, read, write and digest everything that had happened to me during that year. "Let go." was the key phrase that kept coming to mind.

We are used to holding onto everything, so detaching from the past is perhaps the most difficult thing to do concretely and completely.

But if I wanted something new to come in, it was necessary to be brave. I had to take a deep breath and go! I released my tight grip on situations and people that no longer had a place in that moment of my life. I suffered a lot in letting go. I was afraid of having done everything wrong and I felt an unbridgeable void in my life. I had made certain choices and I hoped with all of myself that

that void was filling with an even more powerful light. I didn't know how, where or when, but I trusted that at some point, the light would begin to shine in.

In life things don't happen to you, they happen for you.

Chapter 10

2016 Returning with the Quartet

The trips to Verona for the quartet were a big help in my recovery. In my teammates, I also developed great friendships and it was good to breathe new air and unravel at least part of the fog of those last few months. I still felt out of place and I knew that if I wanted to fully realize myself I had to look elsewhere. I kept working on myself and, despite being confused, I went ahead in searching for my new direction.

At the beginning of the year, I participated in a healing process group called "Family Constellation Meeting" led by Alessandra Garré. I was sitting in a circle in the room full of strangers and Alessandra asked me to describe my mood. I said: "There's something inside of me that doesn't give me peace. I'm in a constant state of agitation and it's as if I always have to chase after something, but I don't know exactly what that is."

Alessandra, very calmly, told me: "Among the people you see here in the room, choose someone to represent your Soul." In all sincerity, I didn't expect that response. I was perplexed, but I trusted her and I chose a girl who then came and stood in the center of the circle. "Now choose a person that represents your Agitation."

I chose a man to whom Alessandra asked: "How are you?"

"I can't give myself peace and I feel like I'm the opposite of her!" He said, pointing to the girl representing my Soul.

"And You, dear Soul, tell me, what do you have to say?" Alessandra asked the girl.

"I am big, very big, huge! I am an Ancient Soul, an artist, I need to express myself and be me again. But now I feel tremendously alone and disconnected from her." She said pointing to me.

I was astounded and petrified witnessing this scene! I had never met that girl before and she didn't know anything about me!

Alessandra looked at me with a motherly smile and told me: "Paola, go to your Soul, reconnect with her. Go on and do not be afraid... Embrace her, she's You."

I couldn't believe what was happening. I breathed and stepped forward in fear, until the girl opened her arms and I could do nothing but throw myself into a liberating cry. It was a warm, sincere and sweet hug. I felt like I had finally come home.

At that point, Alessandra turned to the man who represented my Agitation and asked: "How are you doing?"

"Now I feel better... I feel much calmer." He said sounding relieved.

Alessandra, smiling, continued: "Dear Paola, the only thing you have to do is connect with your true essence. I am sure that sooner or later you will find this connection in a show! Have faith, new horizons will present themselves."

I wanted to ask her a thousand questions but I couldn't! I had to let what had happened settle and simply take it in.

With this new awareness, inspired by that episode, I wrote a poem that speaks of dreams and of the importance of believing in oneself. I recorded my voice along with a piece of music and created choreography for a show in Florence on skates. It ended like this:

It's not what you are that will prevent you from fulfilling
your dreams, but it's what you think you're not...
If you really want to dream, Wake Up!

I wrote the piece mainly for myself but I have presented and shared it with others so that it can be a message of hope and promise for all.

After that group, I perceived the beginning of a new direction, as if I glimpsed a glimmer of light at the end of the tunnel.

In the beginning of 2016, I had entered a book shop to buy a diary. I instinctively selected one that had the image of a dream catcher on the cover, along with the inscription: "Follow your dreams." On the cap of that New Year's champagne bottle I wrote: "Realize yourself" as my resolution for 2016.

I had an urgent need to make a change in my life, and time was running out. "It's now or never!" I said to myself. I didn't know what I was going towards, but I knew I had to renew and restore my energy and be prepared for a call...

In February, I decided to take one of Alessandra's courses in regressive meditation, in a farmhouse in the inland of the Liguria region.

Immediately after the first meditation, I shared what I had seen with another participant and he did the same with me:

"Paola I don't know you but I received a beautiful message for you: there was a butterfly, actually the butterfly was you. You were flying in a garden full of flowers, full of fruits, and you could finally express and be yourself!" He told me with a serene smile. I felt an expansion in my chest and I sensed that that message was genuinely for me! He was not the only one... That weekend, so many things were moving in and around me. Another person suggested that I repeat to myself daily three affirmations with gratitude, like a mantra:

I love and accept myself as I am!
I deserve only the best!
I am worth it!

I did this with constancy and discipline as I had to invest in myself and it was time to welcome every new idea. As it was already happening, however, my unconscious was not playing the same game and was holding me back from change. One morning, I went to yoga, as usual, and towards the end of the class, while moving my leg down from a raised up position, my toes folded all the way back on the non-slip mat. I felt a "crack," an excruciating pain and immediately my little toe began to swell up.

I looked at my teacher Carlotta demoralized and asked her: "Only I can hurt myself doing yoga, can't I?"

And she replied with a shy smile: "Honestly, yes, Paola... I'm so sorry. You probably have to listen to your body more carefully."

A couple of months before I had almost pulled out my back practicing yoga. I was petrified, I couldn't move anymore, my head was spinning and I had been immobile in bed for an hour without being able to even turn.

According to Carlotta, yoga "spoke to me" and it was true, but it's so hard to truly listen to yourself and then have to hear your inner demons. I would have rather not

166

listened and gone forward anyway, but as usual I was immersed deeply in the situation. I was probably too tired, I hadn't taken a day off for months and my body was really feeling it.

In mid-March I would have faced the Italian Championships in the quartet specialty. It was hard even just to walk, let alone skate with my toe in that state! I decided not to get X-rays because, even though I had a feeling it was broken, seeing that wouldn't change anything. I preferred not to know, to try and ignore it. I remember getting hurt on a Thursday morning and the next day, Friday, I had skating Masterclasses in Rome and Naples. I was undecided whether to go or not, but it was all organized already and I couldn't pull out at the last minute. So I took the train carrying some ice with me and had to walk a lot before reaching the hotel. My toe hurt and I was almost positive it was broken.

That weekend was tiring and the pain didn't make it any easier. This is the least pleasant aspect of being self-employed. You can't stop for health problems when you have commitments that involve other people and structures.

I avoided putting on skates for five days but then I had to go to Verona to train. With my foot in that condition, it was really hard. I couldn't handle it anymore! I had started skating again to continue to smile, not to suffer. But my despair reached its peak and a sudden thought flashed through my mind: "Now that's enough! I have always worked hard! I've invested a lot in myself and on my personal growth and I'm tired! It's time for something nice and easy to happen in my life!" I kept repeating it, feeling like I deserved more than my current situation, the stress and the pain.

Sometimes it is necessary to reach your absolute breaking point to make a drastic decision and let yourself feel that you have endured too much and that it's necessary to move forward. It's like a scream coming from deep inside of you and you have to tear off the past in order to show yourself the new light waiting for you in the future.

If you want something new and better to come into your life, sooner or later you will have to make some bold decisions.

A new energy was kindling inside of me and I went forward with confidence and with the feeling that soon I would receive a gift...

On March 8th, while I was waiting for the return train to Genoa in the Verona station, I checked my email box. I had received an email from a lady named Stacey. A little hesitant, thinking it was spam, I decided to open it anyway. It said:

Hi Paola,

I work for Cirque du Soleil casting. We are looking for a character who will play the role of Ela, she must skate and be the emblem of the Free Spirits for the production that will begin next autumn.
We are looking for someone who in addition to athletic skills, has charisma, personality, and above all interpretative skills.
If you are interested contact me at this email address and let's arrange a Skype interview.

I read it several times to make sure it wasn't a joke but it seemed serious! I felt my heart start beating fast and my face lit up instantly! I immediately forwarded the message to my friend Federica, knowing she would support and guide me.

On the train, looking out the window with a different outlook, I remembered that it was International Women's Day. I didn't know yet how things would pan out, but inside, I had a feeling that this was the gift I was waiting for. For the first time, I was witnessing the beginning of a dream that for years always seemed just out of reach. I remember that a smile spontaneously rose from my heart and I uttered a simple but sincere: "Thank you!"

I answered the email as soon as I could, saying that I was interested and I wanted to know more. She wrote to me again that we would have an interview via Skype and, for now, I had to send videos and photos of myself to Cirque du Soleil. I had sent my curriculum vitae just six months before, in a moment of despair in which I tried to see my future in some way. I had done it that way, without paying too much attention. I had launched a hook of hope towards a dream. Now that the possibility had materialized, I was willing to do anything to achieve what at that time was only an invitation.

In the meantime, the Italian Championship for quartets was very close, only a week away. My foot was still hurting and I had to take anti-inflammatory medication. It's not my habit to take medicine, but it was the only way I could get a little relief.

We had trials during the night. Our piece was called Nocturne and we were definitely on theme... We trained from 2:00 AM to 3:00 AM and then again from 6:00 AM to 7:00 AM! It was madness but we had to do it on the rink of the competition, take directions and basically work as much as possible. I was tired, with a sore foot, but I wanted to have this new experience, compete and have fun again.

The official trial went well for my teammates, but not very well for me. The pain in my foot made me dizzy. My energy was scarce, but I knew that I had to clench my teeth again just for three minutes and then I could rest.

There were thirty quartets. The competition for first place was down to us and a quartet from Rome. "Makeup and hair" in four was a lot of fun. We were tired but ready to give it our best. There was tension before the competition, not knowing how it would go. I was watching my teammates warming up, each one with their own habits and I felt so grateful to be back again.

Before starting we hugged each other and entered the rink with determination. During the competition, I realized that I was more focused on my teammates than myself since it was my first time competing with them, but it was probably necessary for blending our energies.

We did well, a high score, the victory was ours! So we secured the transition to the European Championships in Portugal just over a month later, and to the World Championships in Italy for early October. We were happy and this victory gave us good energy to face the following commitments.

Once I got home, I immediately had an X-ray on my foot. Yes, the little toe was fractured! The doctor advised me to stop for a couple of weeks to allow healing and so I did. Two days later I had the highly anticipated interview on Skype with Cirque du Soleil... I was very nervous and hoped to understand English well enough. During the interview, they explained to me what my role would be within the new show: "The character you have to interpret is named "Ela." She is pure energy, she helps others to become better, free people and demonstrate their essence. She goes to "gray people" to wake them up from their torpor and their life so cold and closed. She believes in the importance of helping others with her own positive attitude, with the happiness and joy to live and she sets an example for everyone. She is fire and enthusiasm that is contagious to all human beings."

It was incredible how the character reflected my deepest nature. This was the opportunity that I was waiting for!

Nothing is impossible.
Find yourself, your mission in life and shine.
Others can't help but enjoy
your light and soak up your inspiration!

We must move, act and send energies into the desired direction. We must have the courage to enter inside of ourselves and accept our true selves deeply. We have to inwardly answer key questions such as: what direction does my true essence want me to take? What do I really like? What is the thing that I do well naturally and that gives me the most energy while I'm doing it?

The answer was clear to me. I didn't want to see it because it seemed impossible, but it was evident. "I want to be an artist, I want to skate as a job and I want to create high level performances to continue to express myself; I want to be a pioneer of this artform."

This was what I had asked for and expressed over the years.

I saw it as a distant bright dot, like a star in the sky, but slowly it approached and it became insistent, strong and powerful. I couldn't act anymore as if nothing had happened. I didn't know how to touch that point but I visualized it. I saw myself on a stage, I heard the applause, the energy of the audience and I felt a deep gratitude.

Incredibly, Cirque du Soleil was looking excitedly for a character-skater! It was my chance and I was determined to get that role. I had a week of time to make the two acting videos that they had requested. Luckily Marco was in Genoa that week and he helped me to film and edit them. I was satisfied with the work done. The sixth day, I uploaded them on my profile and with confidence and love I clicked "send." I didn't know when I would get an answer, but every day I kept on visualizing that they would cast me and I thanked them for this incredible opportunity.

At that time, I remember receiving many signs that told me about my new life to come. I was confident. In the meantime, my toe was finally healed and, after two weeks of rest, I resumed training in Verona for the European Championships. While I was living my daily life, I actually stayed focused on the new opportunity that was opening in front of me. I felt that I had to be Ela! I felt that she was calling me.

At the end of April, the European Championships with the quartet went well. We had direct competition with the Portuguese team, and competing in their home was not easy, but we won, despite strong opponents and a really slippery rink.

It was satisfying and great to be recognized as champions, given the sacrifices involved in this training period. Late trains, ongoing trips, no financial support and having to skate even with an injury.

Once the European competition was over, I landed in Milan very early the following day. I only slept three hours and then went directly to the competition area of my athletes. I knew that my presence could be important for them and I wanted to be supportive.

I've always done crazy things for skating, but the vital energy that I had was precisely what made my life extraordinary and I will always be grateful for this.

A week after my return I was invited to an event dedicated to women and their businesses. There were writers, singers, doctors, police officers, sportswomen, and basically anyone who made a difference. I was extremely honored to be part of it.

After the conference, I went for an aperitif with Federica, the first friend I had told about the email from Cirque, and while we were chatting, I received a message from Stacey: "Paola, it is time to discuss. When can I call you?" I showed the message to Federica as I could not believe it! I replied immediately: "Can we chat in an hour?" I wanted to go home where I could count on a better connection. My brother was waiting for me and soon I received the call:

"Paola you have been accepted for the role of Ela! Would you like to take it?"

My hands trembled, my heart started to beat hard and I was incredulous: "Of course I accept it! It's a dream come true! Oh my God, I cannot believe it... Thanks! I'm thrilled!"

Stacey gave me some pointers for the next bureaucratic steps and when I put the phone down I screamed: "They have taken me!!!"

I shared the good news with my family. They were on ecstatic for me! I felt full of energy, happy, excited, but at the same time calm and confident because everything told me that I had found my place, my way.

When we finally manage to desire something without putting filters of doubt, fear, judgment and fault in the middle... What we have asked for takes physical form.

From that day on, my life changed.

It was always me. I did the same things but my attitude was different. Everything was clearer. The previous years had been useful to prepare me for this turning point. My victories, my crisis, my uncertainties, the doubts, the choices I had made and my personal growth had all effected where I was now. I had always seen a stage in front of me and I knew it would be my destination, but I didn't know how to reach it. I had given all of myself and the universe had moved in a way so that everything happened in the best way and most importantly at the right time, when I was ready for it. Furthermore, the sense of uncertainty, the inner torment that always brought me to be looking for something, and never left me in peace, had instantly subsided. I had done so much work on myself. Courses, yoga, visualizations and, along the way, I had often stopped to reflect on my future.

The artist inside of me was kicking and wanted to express herself as soon as possible!

After a long time, I saw the light that would illuminate my new path...

I had decided not to say anything to anyone except for a few close friends, because I didn't know exactly what the upcoming process would be. Did I have to go to the headquarters in October and do another audition? Was it all a definite thing? I didn't have totally clear ideas about what would happen and I preferred to keep the news quiet. I started to train more intensely. Gym every day, water workouts, yoga and of course, skating. I had to be fit for the quartet World Championship in October and after two days I would board the plane for Montreal to begin Cirque on October 12th. All a bit rushed, but also perfectly organized. I could compete, end my career with a World Championship in Italy and then leave for my new adventure! I was definitely a little frightened but I knew it would all work out.

The summer passed quickly but I tried to savor every moment. I spent as much time as possible with my friends and family. I enjoyed the sea, the sunsets and all that made me feel good and at home. I knew I had to fill my soul with love, light and positive energy, because I would need it for the future. I was leaving by myself, headed to a new continent, for a new job and a new lifestyle. This was like nothing I had experienced before and I wanted to anchor myself to my roots to be more confident during my "flight."

September arrived quickly. The World Championships and my departure were approaching. I was training intensely, it was a busy time and I was so excited that I could barely sleep at night.

I always woke up between 4:00 AM and 5:00 AM and I'd lay in my bed looking at the ceiling. I tried to meditate, to breathe, not to think, but sometimes the adrenaline in the body wins. On the other hand, I was about to face my last World Championship. A long cycle was closing and a totally new one was opening. It was a change that marked my life significantly and I was going to embrace it fully.

The World Championships took place in Novara, just two hours from home. My family, friends and some of my athletes, were in the audience cheering me on. Others were watching via the live stream from home.

We were ready to go out there and give it our best. Our purpose was not just to win the title, but to create magic on the rink. We skated to the music of Ezio Bosso. We entered the rink among the last ones and I really wanted to do my best because I knew that, this time, it would be my last competition.

Something magical happened again in my life: after thirty seconds of choreography, I felt that my left skate had come untied! I did not understand what was happening! The feeling was strange but somehow familiar. It was exactly repeating what had happened in Freiburg!

I danced and skated through the entire choreography with my left skate untied. I couldn't believe it! I smiled inwardly as it seemed incredibly unbelievable. Our execution was perfect, the public was mystified and we scored up to a perfect 10!

We were all working together as one energy and the excitement of being on the highest podium again was very strong. I left the rink and went into the changing room to double-check my skate... Undone like in Freiburg! It was a very strong sign for me. The cycle of World Championships had closed the same exact way as it had begun. Still incredulous, with my eyes turned towards the sky I said, "Thank you, really... Thank you!"

I ran out where all of my dear friends and family celebrated and hugged me. I had goosebumps and my emotions were so intense that I could do nothing but smile, and at the same time, cry for joy. My mom said: "Paola, you have the power to transform dreams into reality. Keep it up, fly my little star and never stop." I felt love from everyone and I wanted to get it into my cells and hold onto it forever because a huge chapter of my life was ending.

The next day I finished packing all of my suitcases, I went to say goodbye to some friends and spent as much time as possible with my family.

The emotions inside me became stronger: the joy of the World Championship, the excitement of the departure, the fear of leaving home, the sadness of detaching myself from my family and friends, the tiredness after a year in which I had never stopped... It was so much that in the evening, I burst into tears, unable to cope with it all.

I desperately asked the universe for support and picked up a deck of colored cards gifted to me six months before. Each card contained a message on the back, I picked one with the words:

"Your way is clear, follow it to the end and do not be afraid. We will be by your side."

I smiled and felt a strong heat in my chest. From "up there," someone was guiding me and held my hands to start on this new journey.

Very early the next morning, my family took me to the airport. I was crying, knowing that I would miss my city and all the people dear to me, but I also knew that I had received a call from the other side of the ocean and I had chosen to answer.

On my long flight, I wrote this:

> *It's eight o'clock in the morning and I'm ready to fly, with a bit of melancholy, but with the courage to face and fully enjoy a new chapter of my life with enthusiasm, love and a heart full of gratitude.*

And later I added:

> *... In flight, destination Montreal, Cirque du Soleil! The dream is very close; I can almost touch it. The day before yesterday I won my seventh World Championship, it was an incredible emotion! I'm happy to have chosen this experience because it's made me grow up and it gave me the opportunity to be back in the rink.*

> *I met friends with whom I shared a lot and I had the chance to live a World Championship in Italy with the people who came to support me and have been close to me.*

> *And then, incredible things happen, and every time, in front of all of this, I simply take a step back, breathe and I surrender to the wonders of life.*

During the competition, my left skate was undone, which happened only once before, during the first World Championship in Freiburg. The beginning and the end of a cycle that have filled my life matched. There is a time for everything, we must have the strength to believe that and to never give up. Something bigger takes care of us.

I landed in Montreal, aware that nothing was as it had been and that I would experience an irreversible change.

From the window of my small room, I saw Cirque du Soleil's headquarters and I smiled, like a warrior who conquered a new world after fighting battles for so many years. My past was filling with meaning, everything was needed to bring me there, just at that moment. I had climbed mountains, crossed inner storms to dive into myself and come out again to be able to connect with my soul. I had the courage to let go of what didn't belong to me and to fly, lighter and higher than before.

If we allow life to manifest itself with all of its strength, it can overwhelm us with joy.

Wednesday, October 12th, 2016, I crossed the Cirque du Soleil gate where smiling people were waiting for me. I met my colleagues, my coaches and the artistic directors. Finally, I listened to the whole story of the show and above all, the story behind the character of Ela. She is at the helm of "Free Spirits," free to simply be herself, without prejudice or fear of not being accepted. With her example, she guides people to get out of the "grayness" of life, and to find the original color that truly represents them. Her mission is to help others to find their own path, and she succeeds because she was the first one to do it and knows what it requires.

It seemed exactly like my story! I was a "gray" person too when I was studying physical therapy and I was trying to follow the masses, hiding my talent because I feared it couldn't be sufficiently recognized. I thought that being an artist and living in "color" was impossible! I had silenced my true essence for a long time. Once I understood how to express myself, I rediscovered my creative dimension and I started helping others to do the same. It seemed incredible that Ela's story was so in sync with mine!

Today, more than ever, it is clear to me how much she represents me.

I always try to show others the importance of following their passions, to find themselves and to develop hope and trust. I've been lost and hopeless before and I know what it means to reach your true potential, fully realize yourself and live your dreams. I feel it like achieving these things have been my mission and I want to share that with the world.

We have to take one more step. We have to go beyond
the positive attitude that, in itself, can also become a way
to "settle" and suffer in life if we don't also charge
it with desire, passion and determination.
We are the creators of our existence, one breath after another,
one step after another. We can recognize that in this sense,
we are not inferior to the universal creator.
This can bring down all of the walls of conviction
and resistance and transform our life into a wonderful
experience which can be truly helpful to, and change, others.

The Cirque du Soleil headquarters is incredible! People are all very welcoming, open and smiley. I immediately felt completely accepted and I spent the first three months experimenting with a new way of skating.

It was difficult to skate on such a small stage, but little by little, I gained confidence. I also had many hours of acting training that were really therapeutic. For years, I dreamed of studying acting so intensely and Manon, my teacher, was able to pull so many aspects of my personality out and help me grow artistically and as a human being.

Finally, I was in the right place at the right time, and my state of perpetual restlessness was completely placated. For an instant, from the mountain top, I enjoyed the view. From a state of newly found peace, I was contemplating what laid ahead of me. As I had been told months before, completely unaware that this experience was going to happen: "The butterfly has taken flight towards flourished gardens where she can finally savor the fruits."

Chapter 11

2017 New Life
at Cirque du Soleil

I spent Christmas at home and then I came back to Montreal to continue the creation of the show. I was happy and excited for this new experience, but it scared me a little to know that I would be away from home for a year. I left everything to follow a dream and I didn't know exactly what to expect from this new adventure.

The winter in Montreal was very frigid and it got dark outside very early. The rehearsals would run from 10:00 AM to 10:00 PM and we were indoors all day, without external light, because they had to experiment with the lights suitable for each scene and we would wait for hours for our moment to get on stage.

Endless days were punctuated by pressing rhythms. The lack of light and sun did not help my body to establish a balance between sleep and wakefulness. Every morning I was awake at 5:00 AM and I'd lost the ability to fall asleep. It continued like this for seven months. Because of the cold temperature, the surface of the stage became very slippery. Unable to handle the situation, I was continuously falling down. The narrow space forced me to turn more and, thusly, I was slipping even more. I had to develop a whole new way of skating because the space was a sixth of what I was used to. Also, I couldn't express myself as I desired because I was so focused on not slipping. All of this was incredibly frustrating. The stress increased and I slept less and less. I felt alone, tremendously alone, as if they had torn me from my roots and the wound was still open. At night, I was waking up hugging my pillow looking for consolation.

The cast members were wonderful, but I didn't have the same confidence and friendship with anyone that I felt at home and language barrier made things even more complicated. I was exhausted, but I kept fighting against fears and limitations, because in one way or another, I wanted to get on stage and finally realize my dream.

At the end of February, The *Lion's Den*, the official presentation of the show to all of the leaders of Cirque du Soleil (including founder Guy Laliberté), was held.

The surface of the stage changed every day. I entered for my part and I fell on the floor. I felt really bad. I was ashamed and I considered myself inferior to others and not worthy of the production. I didn't recognize myself anymore. Where was Paola? Mentally strong, determined and sure of what she wanted? I was going through a deep crisis. Impotent and incapable to face the emotional burden, despite the teacher's encouragement, I no longer believed in myself.

After a long wait, I managed to get an appointment with Jean Francois Menard, a World-renowned sports psychologist who helped me to get to the root of the situation: "Paola," he told me, "You're making a big change in your life and as normal, it scares you. You gave up all your certainties to come here and now your resistances are coming to the surface. You must make peace with your unconscious that right now is holding you back."

"Always the same story! But why does it happen? Why is it so hard?"

He looked at me, paused and said: "Because you are looking for perfection, and perfection doesn't exist. You never feel quite good enough."

I froze. He had hit the nail on the head.

He continued: "There is a difference between perfection and excellence. The Perfectionist doesn't accept making mistakes, he is very hard and rigid with himself. If he doesn't make it to the best, it's bad. He feels guilty, and he is ridden with self-doubt. The Excellent, instead, does his best, but he knows he can also make mistakes. He even draws lessons from mistakes and grows thanks to this.

There is no failure, there are lessons from which we can learn. Your perfectionism probably comes from years and years of competing. In fact, an athlete spends a lot of time training to deal with a few competitions a year and making mistakes means throwing a huge amount of work to the wind. Athletes tend to become perfectionists because they have to concentrate to the best of their ability in a single day of competition and they can't afford to make mistakes. Being an artist is different and you must understand and accomplish this passage. Here, you train less and you perform a lot. You will do an average of nine shows a week, more than three hundred shows a year. Before you have trained more and you did five competitions a year.

Do you understand the difference? You can't be a perfectionist, otherwise you will go out of your mind! Things will happen to be wrong and wrong and wrong, and you will have to find a way to shrug them off and realize that tomorrow you will do better. You gave all of yourself at every competition, now you can't afford to do that in every show, otherwise you will burn out after a month. You have to give an average of 75-80% at a show. You have to learn how to dose your strength."

He was right.

I used to be a perfectionist and I didn't allow myself to make mistakes. If, on one hand, this has brought me to very high levels, on the other hand it has provided me with much suffering. I couldn't change my entire way of thinking immediately, but I tried to treasure his words and remember them every day.

In March, we entered the big top for the first time.

It was an incredible: the dream had become a reality.

I went into the dressing room, saw the mirror with my name written on it and I couldn't help but smile and take a picture to capture that moment which was so meaningful. It was March 8th, International Women's Day, the same day, the previous year I received the first email from Cirque du Soleil!

I was really nervous though. Rehearsals at the tent were punctuated by sustained rhythms and by sudden changes. The *solo* I worked on for more than five months was canceled and moved to another act. I had to accept this change exactly two weeks prior to the show's premier and it was an intense challenge both mentally and physically.

I lived in contrasting emotions: I was excited, stressed, happy, exhausted... My body gave me clear signs of blockage. I wasn't able to sleep more than five hours a night, I didn't have my period for five months, I kept losing weight, I had pains in my legs, back and neck and I could only think of the show.

Behind a spectacular performance there is a preparation that often has nothing spectacular about it.

And so, exactly a week before the premier, and one day before the official rehearsal, the blow came!

During a training session on stage, I fell to my face on the ground. It was sudden, strong, I felt a pain in my mouth and I realized that I had broken my two incisors. I couldn't believe it, I immediately thought of my character that represents joy! How could I smile? What would I do? I couldn't even cry or feel any emotion, I was so shocked and alienated. I didn't have the courage to look at myself in the mirror, I was afraid of fainting. Never in my life had something like that happened. I felt like I was living in a nightmare, I had hit rock bottom.

They collected the fragments of my teeth on the stage, put them into milk and brought me immediately to the dentist who managed to fix them back into place with a special adhesive. I felt relieved to see that the result was actually excellent, you could hardly see the conjunction lines.

While returning to the tent by taxi, crossing the city, I was watching the lives of so many normal people that were walking and the children who were leaving school for the day. I realized how much I missed that everyday life. I was really blinded by the evidence, I saw nothing but the big top and my hotel room. I had fought with a smile until that moment, but almost obsessive thoughts began to turn around in my head: "What price I am paying for everything? Is it really worth it? I have left my whole life and all my comforts for this and I am destroyed, a week before the premier."

I was disheartened. The day after, I went to the tent and took part in the first general rehearsal with all of the Cirque du Soleil authorities watching us. I did what I could. I couldn't smile, my mouth hurt, my neck and lumbar area were painful and rigid and the only food I could manage to eat was yogurt.

By a strange coincidence, my brother had a motorcycle accident that same day. They had brought him to the hospital and, waiting for news, I was incredibly worried about him. I couldn't endure any more.

The next day they told me to stay at home and rest. I was sorry not to be there but I felt I really needed it. I finally managed to sleep well and I had an incredible dream: I was alone in the middle of the stage, in the darkness, only a light illuminated me. I looked around, I didn't see anyone.

Suddenly a voice from above began to talk to me:

"Take off your watch." I opened my eyes to the ceiling to see where it came from but I didn't see anything. I took a deep breath, I felt safe. I looked at my wrist and I decided to obey. Hesitating a bit, I took off my watch and I threw it on the ground. "Take off your shoes!" The voice continued. I did it. "Take off your shirt." I didn't know what it meant but with trust I obeyed. He continued: "Take off your skirt."

"Well no! Don't go crazy!" I thought. It seemed too much and I stopped. I waited a minute, no one spoke anymore. I took a deep breath and with hesitation I also took the skirt off. The voice went on: "You see, on stage you have to undress yourself completely, be naked, be yourself without any fiction. You must give what you have to others but you must never forget yourself, your essence, who you are and your value. Nobody will ever take that away from you."

I woke up breathing deeply after that dream. It had felt so real. I opened my eyes and almost couldn't believe the message I had just received. I realized I slept for nine hours in a row. The sun was shining and I was recharged with new energy.

April 20th arrived, the day of the premier, and everyone was very excited to open the show after a very long and difficult period of development. I looked in the mirror and my face seemed really tired. I wished someone from my family or a friend would have been by my side that night, but it wasn't possible. I was happy with what I was doing but I couldn't share this achievement with anyone and I suffered from it.

As much as social media helps us to stay connected, physical and emotional contact with people is crucial.

Despite everything, I felt the support of the coaches who had followed and been with us until that moment. I was ready to get on that so important stage. It was a decisive moment in my career, the transition from athlete to artist represented a turning point and a new life for me.

Volta, the new and current title of the show, means precisely: "Turning the page to realize yourself by manifesting your own authenticity." It's the story of a boy with hair made of blue feathers who is ashamed of being different in this way. Everyone has made fun of him since childhood and throughout his life, he has tried to hide and be a gray person, trying to conform to others. Ela's task is to guide him to find himself, his uniqueness, because what may seem like a problem could be the magic that can instead help you to take off and soar. It's a path of self-acceptance, to learn to love yourself and to regain your own freedom, therefore becoming a Free Spirit. The story is a very strong, contemporary and suitable message for young people.

Being there that evening meant driving myself into a new dimension, having accomplished a transformation. Before the show began, we went all up on stage and Guy Laliberté baptized the Big Top, with the name of "Millennia" for the contemporaneity of the show itself. It was a very intense moment and it gave us great energy to begin. My heart was beating a thousand miles a minute, I was afraid of making mistakes, of falling, of disappointing... rehearsals had never gone well to the end.

I had to do something and so I went to a hidden place to dedicate five minutes to myself. I took a deep breath, closed my eyes and I visualized what I had to do during the show, trying to stay calm and have positive feelings. I thought about the journey I had made and what I had learned to get there in that moment. It was half an hour before the premier. The drawing was made clear in my mind. It hadn't been easy, I had left everything to get to that point, I was out of my comfort zone and I had gone through a deep inner transformation. I had fought my personal battle and I had never given up. Perhaps, for the first time, I felt I really deserved that place and I was proud of what I had achieved. I imagined a light coming from above illuminating me and I prayed to the universe: "Please protect me and give me the strength to do my best, you have guided me so far, take care of me!" From that day every evening, before entering the stage, I imagine a connection between my head and the sky and between my feet and the earth. I feel better, supported by something greater that will never abandon me.

I was backstage warming up and getting into character. I finished my make-up and it was time to put on Ela's costume: it has hair like a lion's mane and it is colorful like a butterfly. I was feeling exactly like that: determined and strong like a lion, but transformed, like a butterfly.

The show began, it was a succession of extraordinary emotions, I tried my best to live in the present. Everything went well and taking our bows at the end was the most intense part for me, as it always was for the award ceremonies after the competitions. The lights, the applause, the people, the energy, the smiles and the tears. At that point the emotions came to the surface and I let myself go after so much tension accumulated. I smiled, I tried to capture every moment of that day and make it mine so it wouldn't go away. We toasted, celebrated and laughed a lot.

It was a magical night that will forever be in my heart.

After the premier, I would have needed a month of vacation to recover from the great amount of physical and emotional stress, but it wasn't possible. Actually, everything was just starting then! The next scheduled break was for a week in late July and it was only April 20th! It was hard to adapt to the rhythms of the show, I was not used to being free in the morning and having to work each afternoon and evening. My sleeping routine didn't improve; I was exhausted but I carried on. I went so far as to perform in horrible condition sometimes, but I felt that I couldn't and didn't want to stop.

I pulled the rope, maybe too much, and I got sick. My body had given me an ultimatum again. The general illness lasted three weeks but I only stopped working for three days. The accumulation of stress from all the events, and from the radical change of life, had manifested. I was looking forward to the next break, we hadn't stopped for seven months. I needed to change air, regenerate and recharge my batteries.

At the end of July, I went to Las Vegas where I slept and I rested for a week. It was the only thing that my body asked me to do and it was the only thing that I could do.

Then, finally, the summer exploded and we resumed the shows at Gatineau. I felt a lot better, I was living in a nice house surrounded by nature with my friend Camilla. The sun was shining and I was skating everywhere. I was feeling good, the public had responded really enthusiastically to the show and I knew I could give more than before.

I love my job. I can't really skate to my full potential because of the narrow space but, being one of the main characters allows me to combine my passion for skating with that of acting.

One of the things that I love the most is the communication with the audience, an integral element of the show. Creating a seamless relationship with the crowd, involving them emotionally, so that they feel part of what is happening on the stage, is essential. This connection is the key to access people's hearts and lead them by hand into the magical world of art and imagination; therefore, it is fundamental to maintain and transmit good energy at all times.

In a performance there must always be love and passion. Where there is art there is emotion. Art is a mission.

The tour continued in Toronto and then moved to the States. The Cirque du Soleil cast is full of wonderful people with big hearts. Friends which I can count on, which is a really important aspect. All of the artists are talented and there is a lot of humility; it seems like I have found people like me. There is no envy or wickedness. On the contrary, mutual support and the desire to have fun reign. We number around forty-five artists in addition to all of the people who work for the show: artistic directors, technicians, cooks, stage managers, tour managers, wives, husbands, fiancées, children... A real little city that moves every two to three months from one place to another. There's a lot of work behind the scenes creating an immense machine that works wonderfully.

One of the things that amazed me the most when I arrived, was to realize that, if you actually are good, you are taken into consideration even at a young age. You can obtain your independence very early and have a career already at twenty-five. It's a reality in America that's very rare in Italy.

Working inside the circus is also interesting from the linguistic and cultural point of view. There are about twenty different nationalities involved and each one brings its own culture. Furthermore, we travel a lot and we have the opportunity to see places that otherwise I would have never known.

It is a unique experience that's making me grow and allows me to learn new things every day.

The stage is a magical place where something sacred happens, where sometimes you are more real than in everyday life. No matter how you feel, if you're fine, if you're angry, happy or sad, the moment you're on stage, you're that character.

In reality, with her positive light, Ela is also a source of inspiration for myself and has helped me so many times to find the strength and the smile even in the hardest moments.

Whenever I think about the beauty we are bringing into the world through this show, I get emotional. To see my face represented on billboards on roads, trucks or on a t-shirt, it's a priceless, joyful feeling. My eyes light up when I see little girls with Ela dolls sitting in the audience.

In these years, far away from home, I grew up establishing a deep connection with myself. I learned to dedicate some space to listen and not to cancel myself out completely for work or for someone else. I managed to enjoy what I was doing and get used to the changes which life had brought me.

Of course there have been difficult moments, times of loneliness and sadness and deeply missing Italy, family and friends. Getting home is always a breath of fresh air, but I feel that for now my place is here.

A few years ago, the doctor saw me performing in New York. Today I can say that I am really "physically here."

This is the tangible proof that I arrived somewhere, that I'm creating something and I'm leaving an indelible mark through my art. I want to continue my mission by following the flow of life, to think big because I learned to do it, and to shine like Ela does, bringing light and color into the lives of others.

Dear Reader,

These tips are here for you to live and practice both your sport and your inner growth with passion, enthusiasm and love...

Put the 10 listed points below into your daily practice. You will get gain confidence and you will evolve to fully express the beauty and talent that belong uniquely to you.

1. Love what you do. Face every situation that presents itself to you with confidence. Nothing happens by chance, everything has a meaning for your personal evolution. Try to understand what that meaning is.

2. If necessary, change your way of thinking. Thoughts are the most powerful tool at our disposal to change reality. Always remember that what you manifest outside, reflects what you have inside.

3. Take some time to be with yourself in solitude. In these moments the warrior in you needs to recover strength for the next challenge. Stay in the present, observe what you feel and what happens around you. Becoming aware cleanses the mind. Recharge yourself by breathing in positive energy and exhaling accumulated tensions.

4. The mind and the body are one. If you neglect one, you stop at half of your potential. Apart from training physically, use the visualization method to train your mind because the brain doesn't distinguish something vividly imagined from something that really happened.

5. Set clear goals with deadlines, but don't stop at this point. Check within yourself if your thoughts and your beliefs are in line with them. You can't achieve something if you do not really believe in it.

6. Humility is the basis of true greatness. It will allow you to understand that you can arrive, but you can also start again, each time to the best of your ability.

7. When a difficulty presents, turn it into a challenge. Your determination can make you overcome every stumbling block.

Instead of: "I can't!" Try telling yourself: "I can!"

8. Listen! Listen to your body, your breath and your heart. Turn off your rational mind for a while and concentrate on your feelings and emotions. Remember that the emotional part always wins over the rational one.

9. Care for your body because it is the tool that allows you to do what you do and be who you are. Respect it, feed it with healthy food, listen to it when it hurts and rest when it asks you to do so.

10. Finally, remember that to Sacrifice means to make something Sacred. Make every activity you believe in sacred, because it is an experience through which you can express the most divine part of yourself.

You are a unique and wonderful human being. It is your duty to express the potential that is in you. Make sure that your dreams become your realities.

I wish that you become a successful, fulfilled and fully realized person.

Paola Fraschini

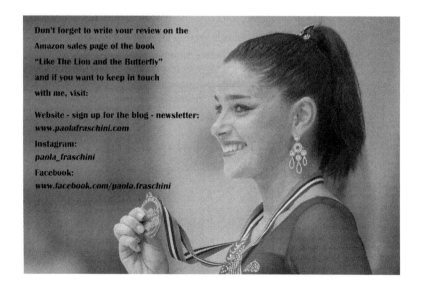

Don't forget to write your review on the Amazon sales page of the book "Like The Lion and the Butterfly" and if you want to keep in touch with me, visit:

Website - sign up for the blog - newsletter:
www.paolafraschini.com

Instagram:
paola_fraschini

Facebook:
www.facebook.com/paola.fraschini

Special Thanks

I would like to thank all of those who have been teachers in life.

My parents, for always believing and allowing me to take flight.

In particular, my mother Laura Bonamico. You have been my coach forever. You transmitted a passion for skating to me and you took me to very high levels with love and dedication. You have always been present at each competition and you guided and supported me in every defeat and every victory. Mom, I'll be grateful for you my entire life!

Thanks dad Renato for the happiness and joy that you give me, for your availability, support and goodness.

An infinite thanks to my brother Matteo for always being there, for all that we have shared since we were born and for the deep love that connects us even remotely.

Thanks to my grandparents. You have been the safe harbor in which I could grow up with a smile.

Thanks Marco. Even if we parted in this life, you've been my partner for an important and long time.

Among my mentors I want to mention:

The doctor, Anna Petritoli, for having pulled me out of the most difficult moments of life and to guide me with the precious teachings mentioned in this book. Thank you for never doubting me.

Max Gentile, for the journey through the years together, for the advice and for helping me to identify my direction in life.

Alessandra Garré, who guided me to the knowledge of a vast spiritual world from which I will never cease to learn.

Jean Francois Menard, sports psychologist of excellence that helped me in my transition from athlete to artist.

Sandro Guerra for the wonderful choreographies created for me.

Carlotta Terranova, my yoga teacher as well as one of my best friends on whom I know I can always count.

Daniela Cirillo, for Rolfing treatments and for the beautiful friendship.

Federica Loredan, for dance, choreography, friendship and mutual support in these years.

Christine Jalbert, healer, Tanja Igrutinovic, astro-healer, Lorena Brunato and Marcella Giuseppini, naturopath. You are all special.

For the realization of the book my gratitude goes to Barbara Zippo for her professionalism, competence and for having guided me in this totally new adventure. Thank you for respecting me, for having to adjust to my time and my crazy life and to have helped me make a dream reality.

Thank you to Federica Bellante Elman for the English translation.

Thanks to Kerry Vera Lea for editing this English version, you're such a talented woman and a generous friend.

I would like to thank my *Cirque du Soleil* family, Volta, with whom I began my life overseas. You are a source of daily inspiration for me and I'm extremely lucky to share this experience with all of you.

I owe a lot to my friends. I won't mention all of your names otherwise I would have to write another book! But know that you are part of it. Thank you for being here.

A tribute goes also to all women: we are the silent force that carries on the world with grace, love and creativity.

And finally, thanks to You who are reading these lines. I hope that the book has been an instrument of light that will brighten up at least a part of your journey. I wish you a great life!

Bibliography
and suggested reads

Bambaren Sergio, *The Dolphin*, Sperling & Kupfer, 1995

Brennan Barbara Ann, *Hands of light*, Bantam, 1990

Brian Tracy, *Maximum Achievement*, Simon & Schuster, 1995

Bourbeau Lisa, *Le cinque ferite e come guarirle*, Amrita 2000

Byrne Rhonda, *The secret*, Atria publishing group, Beyond words publishing, 2006

Cameron Julia *The artist's way: A course in Discovering and Recovering your Creative Self,* Macmillan, 1998

Coelho Paulo, *Manual of the Warrior of Light*, Harper Collins, 1997

Coelho Paulo, *The Alchemist,* Harper Collins, 1988

Dan Millman, *Way of the Peaceful Warrior,* HJ Kramer, 1980

Dyer Wayne, *Change your Thoughts Change your Life*, Hay House UK 2007

Favaretto Andrea, *PNL facile*, Sperling & Kupfer, 2013

Fo Jacopo, *Yoga demenziale*, Fazi Edizioni, 2009

Gentile Max, *Libero di rinascere*, Currenti Calamo, 2017

Hernán Huarache Mamani, *La profezia della Curandera*, Piemme, 2013

Hill Napoleon, *Think and Grow Rich*, Mindpower Press, 2003

Martina Roy, *Emotional Balance*, Hay House, 2010

Martina Roy, *Sei un campione*, Tecniche Nuove, 1998

Rainville Claudia, *Metamedicina*, Ogni sintomo è un messaggio, Amrita, 2000

Redfield James, *The Celestine Prophecy*, Bantam 1993

Ruiz Don Miguel, *The Fourth Agreement*, Amber Allen publishing, 2011

Tolle Eckhart, *The Power of Now*, Yellow Kite, 2001.